Low-Cal
Country

Low-Cal Country

TAKING THE
CALORIES AND CHOLESTEROL
OUT OF
HEARTY COUNTRY COOKING

Louise Dillow

CORONA PUBLISHING CO.
SAN ANTONIO
1992

Cover design by Paul Hudgins

Illustrations by Nancy Moyer

ISBN No. 0-931722-91-8
Library of Congress Catalog Card No. 91-75620

Manufactured in the United States of America
10   9   8   7   6   5   4   3   2   1

Acknowledgements

My special thanks and love go to my six sisters, Inez, Norma, Deenie, Lena, Marie, and Jennie, and several friends who allowed me to rummage through their recipe boxes and cookbooks for country cooking recipes which might lend themselves to the calorie and cholesterol ax.

I wish to thank Doris Curry of A.J. Typewriter Co., for her patience and long-suffering in teaching a computer illiterate like me how to use my word processor, including taking my desperate midnight calls.

My sincere thanks to Kathy Campbell, R.D.-L.D., for her expertise, professional integrity, and patience in calculating calories, cholesterol, fat, and food exchanges in all these recipes. Her consultation has been invaluable in all aspects of writing this recipe book.

My heartfelt thanks and gratitude go to Alice Evett, my copy editor and good friend, for her careful attention to detail. She pointed out to me that I had said "low-fat milk" in twelve different ways.

Last, but not least, I want to thank my publisher, David Bowen of Corona Publishing Company, city-born and -bred, who has not gained a pound since high school, for believing in the importance of a low-cal country cookbook.

Dedication

To my dear husband, Andy Armistead, whose occasional remark, "This doesn't measure up to your usual good cooking," sent the leftovers into the garbage disposal and the recipe into the wastebasket. Andy, who has never dieted a day in his life, approved with gusto the following surviving recipes.

CONTENTS

Low-Cal
Country

Introduction

Folks said that my mother "set a good table." That was back on the farm in Central Texas during the Great Depression. Country people were judged then not by the clothes they wore (and most assuredly not by the *size* of the clothes they wore), not by the car they drove, and not much by the house they lived in. They were judged by whether or not they set a good table.

The table my mother set brimmed over with home-grown vegetables generously seasoned with globs of pork fat, fruit in season suspended in heavy cream, home-cured hams, country sausage, fried chicken and gravy, chicken and dumplings, chilled whole fresh milk, country butter, farm fresh eggs, homemade biscuits, ribbon cane syrup, homemade jellies, cornbread, home-grown potatoes (both Irish and sweet 'taters), fruit cobblers, fried pies, and cakes and pies on Sunday. These were the vittles of my childhood! This was my mother's country cooking.

This is what my folks called "stick to the ribs" food. And stick to the ribs it did—to my ribs, below my ribs, and behind my ribs, slightly further down.

And now the doctor expects me to munch on celery sticks and live on tuna fish packed in spring water for the rest of my life!

The psychiatrist suggests that most weight problems are due to deep-seated emotional deprivations that go back to childhood. Believe me, Doctor, my greatest emotional problem is not due to lack of love and nurturing during my childhood. I had that in abundance—in rich, fattening abundance. My greatest emotional deprivation is that I can no longer eat the down-home country foods like my mother used to cook!

A few years back my sister and I wrote down Mama's previously unwritten recipes and Corona Publishing Company printed them in *Mrs. Blackwell's Heart-of-Texas Cookbook*. There are a lot of mouth-watering recipes in that little book— recipes of foods long forgotten and others best forgotten. They are fabulous and they are fattening!

Now, ten years later, I want to share some more country recipes with you. They are fabulous, but *not* fattening. You see, I lost fifty-seven pounds in six months under the Corsicana Medical Arts weight-loss program. My aim is to keep the weight off. After a lifetime of "setting a good table" not too unlike my mother used to do, I faced the "maintenance period" (meaning the rest of my life) with fear and trepidation.

I like to cook, and I like to entertain. And I have a new husband who loves to eat and never gains a pound. I could see myself becoming one of a large percent who gain back the pounds so painfully, yet proudly, lost. I did not want to return to blood pressure pills, arthritis pills, and a dangerously high cholesterol count. I did not want to go back to waddling when I walked, and not being able to bend down to tie the shoelaces on my brand new Reeboks. I did not want to start letting the seams out on my new wardrobe.

I did not want to prepare two separate menus, a his and hers, for every meal. And I did not want to return to the roller-coaster ride of dieting and splurging, more dieting and splurging, followed by guilt and depression, and more splurging to ease the depression.

It finally became clear what I had to do. I decided to cook and serve the same kind of foods I'd always served. I would just take the calories and cholesterol out. And that is what Kathy Campbell and I have done. We have taken the calories out of country cooking.

Kathy Campbell is a Registered Dietitian and Nutrition Consultant to the Corsicana Medical Arts Clinic Weight Reduction Program. She has calculated the calories and cholesterol count of the recipes by the use of N-Square Computing, Nutritionist III Analytic software, and by reading labels of some of the newer prepared food. In most cases, the calculation was rounded to the nearest whole number.

Kathy has been unyielding in not letting me help you cheat, not even a little bit. As you know, all of us with weight problems are notorious for cheating when it comes to counting calories. (The doctor calls it denial. I call it cheating.) I tried to get by without counting the flour on a dough board, or the milk in which chicken was marinated, or the measly number of calories in a teaspoon of vanilla extract. No luck! Kathy caught me every time.

The recipes in this book were designed for weight maintenance, yours and mine, whether you have lost ten pounds or one hundred and ten. They are also suitable for those interested in a steady weight loss. All are under 300 calories, with a large number being around one hundred calories or less. In addition to weight maintenance, Kathy and I are very concerned about cholesterol. We are even more concerned about saturated fats and hydrogenated fats, which cause cholesterol build-up in the body even though they may not themselves contain cholesterol. For that reason, all of the recipes are not only low in cholesterol (except some of the fish recipes) but are also low in saturated fat. Furthermore, in the main we have refrained from using products containing palm oil, coconut oil, and hydrogenated fat except that which might be found naturally in some meats.

Kathy calculated the recipes according to calories, fat, cholesterol, and saturated fat. She also broke them down into food exchanges for diabetics and others whose diet requires that approach.

Kathy and I are not unconcerned about how much salt you are consuming. Although we have not given you a read-out on the amount of sodium in each recipe, we have lowered the salt in most of them. You will have to use your own judgment and your doctor's advice in regard to how many shakes your saltshaker shakes.

These recipes, sans excessive calories, are so tasty that my dad, if he were alive today, would smack his lips and declare as he often did of my mother's cooking, "Now, that's what I call 'larrupin' good."

You and I are going to eat well without guilt and without martyrdom and without putting the weight back on. Our families, for the most part, are going to eat right along with us and be the healthier for it.

There are many new products on the market now, developed to help people like us reduce calories and cholesterol without sacrificing looks and taste. All it takes is a little time and creativity and a snapshot of the "old you" you want to find again, or a magazine cut-out of the projected "new you" on the refrigerator door. Instead of the perennial concern about dieting, we are going to concern ourselves with a new way of cooking.

This is as good a time as any to give you my opinion about the controversy regarding the use of 'artificial and/or chemical products.' One or two of my friends (skinny friends that is) have said, "Why, I wouldn't have those sweeteners with all those chemicals in my house."

"Chemicals" is not a dirty word. What do they think that baking soda is? It is a chemical, a highly respected chemical that has been around in the United States for over one hundred and forty years. It says so on the box. It took the place of potash and pearl ash as a leavening agent for baking. I'm grateful to that fine old company that manufactures baking soda.

I'm even grateful that I can bite into an apple without finding *half* a worm, and that my spinach isn't covered with those little black bugs. Remember, I'm from the country. I know about such things. Believe me, the foods you buy in the supermarket have very little resemblance to their original natural state before interference by man and/or man-made chemicals. For instance, Old Bossy does not give pasteurized, homogenized milk with Vitamin D added. Nor does she give 1%, 2%, or skim milk. I'm grateful for the man-made compulsory immunization laws of the 1930's which prevent her from giving milk with tuberculin bacteria in it.

I'm also grateful for the man-made products with which we can sweeten our tea or coffee, and with which we can bake an occasional dessert without adding so many calories. I'm grateful to be able to enjoy the sugar-free colas and chewing gum.

Some of the sweeteners have a required statement on the

box saying that "this product may be hazardous to your health . . . because saccharin has been determined to cause cancer in laboratory animals." That bothers me a bit. I'm more bothered, however, to read from the *Physician's Desk Reference* that the blood pressure pills and the arthritis pills I was taking before I lost 57 pounds had warning signs a page long, including the risk of congestive heart failure, renal disease, liver disease, stomach problems, and many other problems that I can't spell let alone pronounce. These side effects have turned up in people, not just in laboratory animals. Given all these warnings, I would take these pills again, if the need should arise.

I do not mean to be flippant about the Food and Drug Administration's efforts to protect us. The point of all this digression is to say that life is a trade-off.

Any person who is capable of reading this book has read and been told dozens of times that obesity may cause strokes, heart attacks, diabetes, arthritis, back problems, and foot problems. The question, then, becomes: Which is more hazardous to your health—obesity or some of the artificial products to aid you in your constant battle with obesity?

Preparatory to writing this book, I went up and down the aisles of my favorite supermarket reading labels, making comparisons. I have fingered so many brands of artificial sweeteners, oils, salad dressings, milk products, cheese, condiments, and margarine that when I go into a store, I imagine the store manager will come up behind me and say, "Madam, please don't squeeze the margarine."

Speaking of labels, let me give you a hint or two which Kathy has taught me: You'd best read the fine print even if you have to use your binoculars to decipher it. Fine print is like your teenager's whisper. The finer the print, or the lower the whisper, the more reason to look and listen hard. A case in point is the ever increasing "No Cholesterol" labelling on many products. Read on, and on, and on *some more*. Look out for palm oil and coconut oil and other products high in saturated fats, as well as hydrogenated oils that have a cholesterol-raising effect in the body. In your perusing of fine print, look also for sodium content in prepared food.

Occasionally, in the pages that follow, I have used brand names. This is not to be construed as an official endorsement. By the time you read this, in all likelihood there will be many more improved products on the market. My store manager tells me that new products are coming in almost daily. Get that label habit. Remember when the net weight of the product was all that was required on the label? Public demand now requires, not so much the *product's* net weight, but what the product is going to do to *our* net weight.

Although it has been over a half century since I lived down on the farm, these recipes are basically country fare. Since leaving the farm, I have lived in several towns in Texas, on the Texas-Mexican border, the Texas Gulf Coast, and several cities up north, including the Washington, D.C. area. During that time I picked up a few city ways. I also developed an appreciation of regional foods. You will notice that I have sprinkled in a little Minnesota wild rice, Chesapeake Bay Crab, Illinois dumplings, New England clam chowder, Cleveland sour cream, and Mexican mole among the chicken-fried steak, black-eyed peas, and cornbread.

Enjoy. Eat well. Be happy.

Soups

SOUPS

There are times in our lives when nothing, but nothing, will take the place of a steaming bowl of homemade soup— like on a cold rainy day when the whole world looks damp and dreary and forlorn; like when you are coming down with a cold and are too sick to eat, but not sick enough to stay home from work; or when you are sick from worry and solid food refuses to go past your Adam's apple to take the place of that lump in the pit of your stomach. That's when you need homemade soup! There are other times when soup hits the spot too, when you simply want a quick light lunch, or a one-dish supper.

There is no way to make a little bit of soup. Go ahead. Make a large pot. Take some to a sick friend. A Crockpot of vegetable or chicken soup is the nicest thing you can possibly take to a person who has just lost a loved one. If you do not have a sick or bereaved friend to share your soup with, freeze all the soup that your family will not eat in about three days. I freeze it in individual servings. It sure is handy when you've come in out of the cold and you don't have a cooked meal waiting for you.

Since we are counting calories and cholesterol, I have measured the ingredients for the soup recipes. I must confess that this the very first — and I suspect it will be the last—time I have ever measured ingredients for soup. You have my permission to take the same liberties which I do, provided that you skim off all fat from the stock before using it, and that you do not use a heavy hand in adding the noodles or potatoes.

Jky

Cream of Broccoli Soup

1 cup broccoli, 1/2-inch flowerets
1 Tbs. low-fat margarine
1 cup skim milk
1/2 cup canned evaporated skim milk, undiluted
6 oz. processed cheese, reduced fat
1 Tbs. cornstarch
1 tsp. chicken bouillon granules
1/8 tsp. ground allspice

Steam broccoli until tender. I use my special microwave steamer for this purpose, but it can be done on top of the stove.

Place margarine in a nonstick skillet or saucepan. Melt margarine and add cornstarch. Stir in milk and canned milk, stirring until well blended. Add chicken bouillon granules, and allspice. Cook until thickened. Add cheese and stir until melted. Take one cup of mixture, add with broccoli, and blend in electric blender for 30 seconds. Return to pot with remainder of ingredients and simmer until well heated. Do not boil. The use of a blender is not absolutely necessary, but tends to make it lighter.

4 Servings: 182 Calories per Serving; 8 grams Fat; 21 mg. Cholesterol; 4 grams Saturated Fat.

Food Exchanges: 1 meat; 1/2 bread; 1 fat; 1/2 milk.

Cream of Tomato Soup

1 can (46 oz.) tomato juice, divided
1 cup nonfat dry milk
2 Tbs. minced onion flakes
2 Tbs. chopped fresh parsley
2 tsp. white vinegar
1/2 tsp. sweet basil
1/2 tsp. salt
1 bay leaf
2 whole cloves
1 pkt. Sweet'n Low

Put powdered milk in a bowl. Gradually add 1-1/2 cups of the tomato juice, and blend. Set aside. In a large saucepan, combine remaining tomato juice and other ingredients, except Sweet'n Low, and simmer about five minutes. Remove bay leaf and cloves. Pour some of the hot liquid into the tomato–milk paste. Blend well. Pour mixture back into saucepan. Heat slowly, stirring constantly, to serving temperature. Do not boil. Stir in Sweet'n Low, and serve immediately.

6 Servings: 81 Calories per Serving; 0 Fat; 0 Cholesterol; .08 grams Saturated Fat.

Food Exchanges: 2 vegetables; 1/2 milk.

Fresh Vegetable Soup

1 qt. tomatoes, peeled, fresh, or canned
1 large onion, chopped
2 carrots, chopped
1 clove garlic
1 cup celery, diced
2 medium potatoes, diced
1/2 cup butter beans, English peas, or green beans
2 pods green pepper, chopped
1/2 cup okra, sliced
1/2 cup corn, fresh or frozen
1-1/2 qts. water
1 tsp. salt
1 tsp. black pepper
5 whole cloves
2 cups chicken or beef broth, fat skimmed from the
    top
1/2 cup noodles, uncooked

Mix water and broth in a large stockpot. Add vegetables and seasoning. Cook slowly for about 45 minutes. Add the noodles and cook another 30 or 40 minutes. This makes a marvelous rainy or chilly day meal. Serve with cornbread or crackers.

10 Servings: 109 Calories per Serving; 1 gram Fat; 10 mg. Cholesterol; .09 grams Saturated Fat.

Food Exchanges: 1 bread; 1-1/2 vegetables.

Soup

Garden Vegetable Soup

2 cans (16 oz.) whole tomatoes
1 qt. water
1/2 lb. okra, sliced
1/2 lb. green beans
1 large onion
2 stalks celery
2 carrots
1-1/2 cups cabbage, coarsely chopped
1/2 tsp. salt
1/2 tsp. dried parsley flakes
1/2 tsp. black pepper
1/2 tsp. onion powder
2 cloves garlic

Combine all ingredients in large pot. Cover and simmer for 1-1/2 hours.

11 Servings, one cup each: 46 Calories per Serving; 0 Fat; 0 Cholesterol; .07 grams Saturated Fat.

Food Exchanges: 2 vegetables.

Gazpacho

Now I know that you are not likely to find gazpacho on the menu at your average country-cooking restaurant. Not until after some of the restauranteurs have seen this book, that is. All of the ingredients, except the condiments, come right out of the garden. It may not be "country", but this recipe came from Peggy Campbell who always serves gazpacho in her summer "country home" when her senior citizen swimming group, called the Mermaids, goes there for lunch and a swim. Come to think of it, the first time I had gazpacho was at a hacienda turned country inn for American tourists, outside Saltillo, Mexico.

> 1 (46 oz.) can tomato juice
> 5 beef bouillon cubes
> 4 to 5 medium tomatoes, chopped
> 1 cup celery, chopped
> 1/2 cup bell pepper, chopped
> 1/2 cup green onions, chopped
> 1 cucumber, chopped
> 1 clove of garlic, crushed
> 8 Tbs. red wine vinegar
> 1 Tbs. Worcestershire sauce
> 1/4 tsp. Tabasco sauce

Dissolve bouillon cube in 1 cup of hot tomato juice. Stir in all ingredients and chill overnight. Serve cold in cups or punch cups with low-salt crackers.

18 Servings of 3/4 cup per serving: 21 Calories per Serving; 0 Fat; 0 Cholesterol; 0 Saturated Fat.

Food Exchanges: 1/2 vegetable.

Hearty Beef Soup

1 lb. ground lean beef
2 garlic cloves
1 cup chopped onion
1 cup carrot chunks
1 cup celery, chopped
5 beef bouillon cubes
1/4 cup rice, uncooked
2 cans (15 oz.) tomatoes
3-1/2 cups water
1 can (15 oz.) kidney beans
Pepper to taste
1/2 tsp. basil
1 can (15 oz.) cut green beans
1 cup okra, thick sliced (optional)
Salt to taste

Brown ground meat and onions in nonstick skillet. Transfer to a large pot and add all other ingredients. Bring to a boil. Cover and simmer for about one hour. You may prefer to add okra pieces during the last 15 minutes.

12 Servings: 173 Calories per Serving; 4.5 grams Fat; 33 mg. Cholesterol; 2 grams Saturated Fat.

Food Exchanges: 1-1/2 meat; 2/3 bread; 1-1/2 vegetable.

—— Mock Cream of Mushroom Soup ——

1 can mushrooms with liquid
1/2 cup nonfat dry milk
1 cup water
1 envelope beef bouillon
Salt and pepper to taste

Blend all ingredients in electric blender until smooth and creamy. Heat and serve.

2 Servings: 62 Calories per Serving; 0 Fat; 0 Cholesterol; .04 grams Saturated Fat.

Food Exchanges: 1 milk.

—————— Quick Corn Chowder ——————

1 can Weight Watchers cream of mushroom soup
1 No. 2 can (2-1/2 cups) whole kernel corn
2 cups skim milk
1 small onion
1 tsp. low-fat margarine
1/2 tsp. Molly McButter
1/4 tsp. salt
Pepper to taste

Sauté onions in margarine in a Teflon skillet. Combine soup, corn, and milk. Add salt and pepper. Simmer for 15 minutes. Serve immediately.

6 Servings of 1 Cup each: 132 Calories per Serving: 0.5 Fat; 0 Cholesterol; 0.4 grams Saturated Fat.

Food Exchanges: 1 bread; 1 milk.

—— Riffle Soup (Egg Dumplings) ——

1/8 cup egg substitute
1/4 tsp. salt
1 Tbs. water
1-1/2 cups flour
3 cups chicken broth

Add salt and water to egg substitute. Mix in flour. Dough should be very stiff—too stiff to roll out on board. Pinch off pieces about the size of a butter bean, and drop in boiling broth. Reduce heat to moderate and cook for twenty minutes. This is the Southern Illinois country version of Jewish Mother's chicken soup.

6 Servings: 143 Calories per Serving; 2 grams Fat; 0.7 mg. Cholesterol; 0 Saturated Fat.

Food Exchanges: 1/2 meat; 1-1/2 bread.

—— WASP Mother's Chicken Soup ——

This is what I take to my friends who are sick, or blue, or who have lost a loved one.

3 chicken breast halves
10 cups water
2/3 cup onion, coarsely chopped
2/3 cup celery, coarsely chopped
1 small Irish potato
1/2 sweet potato
2 carrots, chopped in one-inch pieces
1 cup cabbage, coarsely chopped
1 tsp. sweet basil
3 fresh parsley leaves, or 1 tsp. dried

1/2 tsp. salt
1 tsp. black pepper
1 cube chicken bouillon
Homemade noodles (See recipe below)

Boil three chicken breasts that have been skinned and defatted, in 10 cups of water in a large pot until tender. Take out the chicken, debone it, and cut it up in large bite-size pieces. Add bouillon cube.

Add cabbage, celery, onion, carrots, Irish potato chunks, and sweet potato chunks. Add basil, parsley, pepper, and salt. Cook for about thirty minutes. Add homemade noodles slowly so that boiling will not subside. Then add chicken pieces and cook for another 35 or 40 minutes with lid somewhat ajar on the pot. Watch carefully as chicken is likely to boil over.

Homemade Noodles

1/4 cup frozen egg substitute, thawed
1 Tbs. plus 1 tsp. water
1/2 tsp. salt
1 cup flour plus 2 Tbs. flour for the board

Beat egg substitute, salt, and water together. Add flour gradually and mix, forming a ball. The dough will be very stiff. Place between two sheets of wax paper and roll out as thin as possible. I have a little noodle-cutter gadget which I've had for forty years, but I have not seen one on the gadget shelves for many years. You can use a pizza roller or a sharp knife to cut the strips. My daughter-in-law has a pasta attachment to her food processor, but that is for serious pasta makers.

8 Servings: 163 Calories per Serving; 2 grams Fat; 27 mg. Cholesterol; 0 Saturated Fat.

Food Exchanges: 1 meat; 1 bread; 1 vegetable.

Ultra-Lite Clam Chowder

1 can (4 oz.) mushrooms
1 small bottle clam broth
1 can minced clams
1/2 cup skim milk
1/4 tsp. salt
1/4 tsp. pepper
1 tsp. minced dried onion
1 Tbs. cornstarch

Blend mushrooms, clam juice, and milk in blender. Pour into a saucepan. Add one tablespoon of cornstarch and blend well. Cook until mixture begins to thicken slightly. Add minced clams, salt, and pepper. Continue cooking until completely heated.

3 Servings: 45 Calories per Serving; 1 gram Fat; 18 mg. Cholesterol; 0 Saturated Fat.

Food Exchanges: 1 meat.

Cape Cod Clam Chowder

1 can Weight Watchers mushroom soup
1 can (6-1/2 oz.) minced clams
2 cups skim milk
1 cup water
3 medium-size potatoes, boiled and cubed
2 tsp. minced onion flakes
1 tsp. margarine, low-fat

2 tsp. powdered butter flavoring (Butter Buds or
    Molly McButter)
1/2 tsp. celery salt

Gradually add water to mushroom soup and stir to make smooth. Add all other ingredients. Blend well. Heat slowly to serving temperature, stirring constantly. Serve hot.

6 Servings of 1 cup: 121 Calories per Serving; 1 gram Fat; 21 mg. Cholesterol; 0.3 grams Saturated Fat.

Food Exchanges: 1/2 meat; 1 bread; 1/2 milk.

——— New England Clam Chowder ———

3 medium-size potatoes (about 1 lb.)
1 large onion
2 cups water
1 bay leaf
1/2 tsp. celery salt
1/4 tsp. pepper
1 qt. skim milk
3 Tbs. cornstarch
2 pkgs. Butter Buds
2 cans (6-1/2 oz. each) minced clams
Chopped chives

Peel and dice potatoes and onion and place in a large saucepan along with water, bay leaf, celery salt, and pepper. Boil gently until potatoes are tender— 15 to 20 minutes. Reduce heat to simmering. Combine milk, cornstarch, and Butter Buds, and add slowly to potato mixture, stirring constantly. Add clams and juice and stir over medium heat until soup begins to boil and thicken slightly. You may mash some of the potato pieces up against the side of the pan to add more thickening. Reduce heat and simmer 5 minutes. Remove bay leaf and garnish with chopped chives before serving.

8 Servings of one full cup each: 147 Calories per Serving; 5 grams Fat; 34 mg. Cholesterol; 1 gram Saturated Fat.

Food Exchanges: 1/2 meat; 1 bread; 1 milk.

Oyster Stew

1 pint oysters with liquid
3 cups skim milk
2 tsp. Butter Buds
Pepper
Salt

Pour oysters with liquid into a stew pan. Cook over medium heat until oysters begin to curl slightly. Add milk, salt, pepper, and Butter Buds. Heat until milk just barely reaches boiling point. Serve immediately.

Serves 5: 121 Calories per Serving; 3 grams Fat; 57 mg. Cholesterol; 0.8 grams Saturated Fat.

Food Exchanges: 1 meat; 1/2 milk; 1/2 fat.

Ivy

Vegetarian Chili

1-1/2 cups cooked pinto beans, with liquid to
   make 2 cups
1 medium onion
2 cloves of garlic
1 can (15. oz.) tomatoes, with liquid
1 large carrot, grated
1 zucchini, peeled and finely chopped
1 yellow squash, chopped
1/2 cup canned mushrooms
1 tsp. olive oil
4 tsp. chili powder
1/2 tsp. cayenne pepper
1/2 tsp. garlic salt
1 tsp. sweet basil
1/2 jalapeño, chopped
1/2 tsp. celery salt

Sauté chopped onion and minced garlic in 1 tsp. of olive oil,
until onions are clear. Cook carrots, zucchini, and yellow squash
in water to cover.

When vegetables are soft, add cooked onion, canned tomatoes, and mushrooms. Add jalapeño and spices. Then add cooked
pinto beans. Cook until all are blended and mixture is piping hot.
You may need to add additional water.

*6 Servings: 127 Calories per Serving; 0 Fat; 0 Cholesterol;
0 grams Saturated Fat.*

Food Exchanges: 1 bread; 2 vegetables.

Iky

Vegetable—Bean Soup

1/3 cup dried navy beans, uncooked
2 qts. water
3 carrots, diced
3 medium tomatoes, peeled and chopped
3 small onions
2 stalks celery
2 cloves garlic
3 Tbs. olive oil *— leave out*
Pinch of ground savory
Salt
Pepper

Wash beans thoroughly. Place in large pot. Add water and bring to a boil. Remove from heat. Cover and let sit for an hour or so. Return pot to heat and let water come to a boil. Reduce heat and simmer for 45 minutes. Add remaining ingredients. Simmer, uncovered, for 35 to 40 minutes, or until beans are tender.

8 Servings: 82 Calories per Serving; 5 grams Fat; 0 Cholesterol; 0.8 grams Saturated Fat.

Food Exchanges: 1 bread.

Salads

SALADS

Salads are great for calorie- and cholesterol-watching. Most are attractive, tasty, and easy to prepare. But do not fall into the trap of thinking that all salads are slimming.

You have seen fat men in restaurants nobly order a chef's salad while their companions ordered steak, only to drown the crisp vitamin-filled greens with globs of Roquefort dressing. These same men ask for extra garlic bread sticks, and dump three spoons of sugar in their coffee. You have also gone out to lunch with ladies who declared that they were watching their calories and would simply opt for the salad bar. Then they pile the salad plate high with fried chicken livers or wings, canned peaches, or fruit salad with tiny bits of fruit suspended in mountains of whipped cream, pour salad dressing over the few greens they select, and then sprinkle sunflower seeds or pine nuts over the whole bit. Some of them later sneak back for a dish of fruit cobbler.

The country cooking of my childhood did not include many salads, except potato salad, wilted lettuce, and cooked English pea salad. In season, we had lots of sliced tomatoes, cucumbers in vinegar, green onions, radishes, sliced onions, and green peppers. We would not think of eating raw broccoli, cauliflower, or turnips. Why, I was shocked when Scarlett O'Hara ate a raw turnip right out in the field as she vowed she would never let her family go hungry again. And looking back on it, I do not believe that Scarlett had any Hidden Valley buttermilk dressing to dip the turnip in.

I have not included recipes for simple green salads and fruit salads. If you are like most people I know, you will use whatever is in the refrigerator. If you like the Fifties-style salad made with a canned peach, pear, apricot, or pineapple over a lettuce leaf, with a dollop of mayonnaise and cheese or cherry on top, be sure to stay away from fruit canned in heavy syrup. Instead, use "light" fruit, reduced calorie mayonnaise, or low-calorie cottage cheese, and skip the cherry or cheese on top. If you want to add a touch of color, put three raisins or a small triangle of unpeeled apple on top. If you make a mixed fruit salad like ambrosia, skip the coconut, walnuts, and marshmallows. You can use a few drops of coconut extract and walnut extract, and cottage cheese. For the tossed green salad, just say no to the avocado. Use cantaloupe chunks in the summertime and grapefruit segments in the winter, and you can add a little jicama for variety.

Jicama (pronounced *he*-ka-ma) is an interesting vegetable now found in most supermarkets. I was introduced to it when I moved to the Texas–Mexican border. It is an ugly looking thing, about twice the size of a rutabaga, slightly misshapen, with a tough brown skin, not covered with wax as the rutabaga. The inside of the jicama is not too unlike a turnip in texture and in taste. It is sometimes known as a Mexican Yam.

Until recently, I served jicama only as a raw vegetable like a carrot stick to eat by itself or with dip. Then I heard a man on television talk about jicama. He said there are only 20 calories in a cup of jicama, and that you can cook it and use it as a substitute for water chestnuts in salads and casseroles. He's right!

To cook jicama, slice it in small bite-size pieces and sauté it in a Pam-sprayed Teflon skillet. Pour one-fourth cup of water in the skillet. Sautéed jicama can be frozen for later use.

Instead of giving you specific measured-out recipes for green salads, I think it will be more helpful to give you the calories of the usual ingredients for green salad, along with a few helpful hints.

Unless you add a lot of fattening extras, you can have a large bowl of green salad with very few calories. There are some excellent low-cal salad dressings on the market which no longer taste like castor oil as they formerly did. There are also several mixes in dry form with as little as two calories per serving. Use only a minimum amount of vegetable or olive oil, then fill in with water and vinegar.

First of all, have the lettuce crisp, by using a lettuce crisper for iceberg lettuce. For leaf lettuce, wash and pat almost dry with a towel. Place in a plastic bag before putting in the refrigerator. Always tear the lettuce instead of cutting it. Add tomatoes just before serving. Add salad dressing for individual servings if you expect to have some greens left over. The leftover vegetables will remain crisp if placed in a Tupperware or similar bowl and can be used the following day.

For twenty-five calories for the whole bowl, you can add a gourmet touch by sprinkling one tablespoon of Parmesan cheese over the green salad.

A green salad is not only low in calories and high in vitamins, but it takes a long time to eat it, thus serving the satiation need.

These are the salad vegetables. Mix and match as you like.

Vegetable	Amount	Calories
Iceberg lettuce	1 cup	05
Boston lettuce	1 head	25
Endive	1 cup	10
Romaine lettuce	1 cup	10
Broccoli	1 cup	40
Cabbage	1 cup	15
Cucumbers	6 large	05
Cauliflower	1 cup	31
Carrot	1	30
Bell pepper	1	15
Celery	1 cup	20
Green onions	6	15
Mature onion	1 cup, sliced	45
Mushrooms	1 cup	20
Squash	1 cup	30
Spinach	1 cup	15
Radishes	4	05
Tomatoes	1 medium	25
Grapefruit	1/2	50
Cantaloupe	1/2	80
Avocado*	1	370

*You can see why I am omitting avocado in my recipes.

Amy

Apple-Cabbage Salad

2 cups coarsely grated cabbage
2 medium apples
1 cup carrots, coarsely grated
1 cup pineapple chunks, unsweetened, drained
1/4 cup Miracle Whip, Light
2 Tbs. yogurt, low calorie
1/4 tsp. ginger

Wash, core, and chop unpeeled apple into 1/2-inch cubes. Combine cabbage, apples, carrots, and pineapple. Combine mayonnaise and yogurt. Blend mayonnaise mixture with fruit and vegetables. This is better if it is refrigerated for one or two hours.

8 Servings: 57 Calories per Serving; 1.5 grams Fat; 1 mg. Cholesterol; 0 Saturated Fat.

Food Exchanges: 1 fruit; 1 vegetable.

Applesauce Jello Salad

2 cups applesauce (no sugar added)
2 pkgs. (3 oz.) raspberry Jello, sugar-free
1 cup unsweetened orange juice
7 oz. Diet 7-Up

Heat applesauce. Dissolve raspberrry Jello in the hot applesauce. Stir in the orange juice. Carefully pour in the Diet 7-Up. Chill. Pour into a mold or an 8x8" cake pan or casserole dish.

6 Servings: 65 Calories per Serving; 0 Fat; 0 Cholesterol; 0 Saturated Fat.

Food Exchanges: 1 fruit.

Possible

Corn Salad

    1 can (12 oz.) whole kernel corn, drained
    1 tomato
    1/4 cup bell pepper, chopped
    1/4 cup onion, chopped
    3 Tbs. pimiento
    1/4 tsp. salt
    1/4 cup tomato juice
    2 Tbs. Miracle Whip, Light
    2 Tbs. red wine vinegar
    1/2 tsp. celery seed
    1/4 tsp. dry mustard
    1/4 tsp. pepper
    1/2 tsp. dill weed
    1 pkt. sweetener

Mix all vegetables together in salad bowl. Combine tomato juice, mayonnaise, vinegar, sweetener, and seasonings. Mix with vegetables. Refrigerate overnight.

6 Servings: 65 Calories per Serving; 1.5 grams Fat; 1 mg. Cholesterol; 0 Saturated Fat.

Food Exchanges: 1 bread; 1 vegetable.

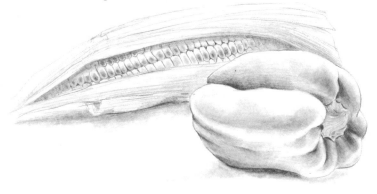

Sounds good -holidays

—————— Cranberry Relish ——————

1 lb. cranberries
1 tsp. sweetener
2 Tbs. sugar
1 cup seedless raisins
1/2 cup orange juice
1 Tbs. grated lemon peel
2 Tbs. lemon juice
1/2 tsp. cinnamon
1/2 tsp. cloves
1/2 tsp. allspice

Put cranberries through food chopper, using coarse blade. Mix all ingredients. Chill one hour or more to blend flavors. Makes about 3-1/2 cups. Can be stored in freezer. This is an excellent relish to be served with poultry or meat. A small jar of this would be great to go in a Christmas basket for friends.

28 Servings at 1/8 cup per Serving: 20 Calories per Serving; 0 Fat; 0 Cholesterol; 0 Saturated Fat.

Food Exchanges: 1/4 fruit.

– Crispy Green Beans and Spuds Salad –

1/2 lb. new red potatoes
1 lb. fresh green beans
1 Tbs. olive oil
1 Tbs. white wine vinegar
1 Tbs. water
1/2 tsp. salt

1/8 tsp. garlic powder
1/4 tsp. pepper
Lettuce leaves

Wash potatoes but do not peel; cook in boiling water, covered, for about 10 to 15 minutes. Do not overcook to the point of mushiness. Drain potatoes and set aside.

Wash beans. Trim ends and remove strings. Instead of snapping the beans, cut them with a sharp knife into 1- and 1/2-inch lengths. Cover with water and bring to a boil. Reduce heat, cover, and simmer 8 minutes. Southern folks may want to cook them a little longer, and Northerners a little less.

Cube the potatoes in bite-size pieces, leaving the skins intact. Combine potatoes and beans, tossing lightly. Combine the oil, vinegar, water, salt, garlic powder, and pepper, stirring well. Pour over the vegetables. Cover and chill for at least four hours. Serve on lettuce cups, or put in a lettuce-leaf-lined salad bowl and serve.

6 Servings: 79 Calories per Serving; 3 grams Fat; 0 Cholesterol; 1 gram Saturated Fat.

Food Exchanges: 1/2 bread; 1 vegetable; 1/2 fat.

——————— Cole Slaw ———————

2 cups shredded cabbage
1 gherkin sweet pickle
1/2 bell pepper
1/4 cup onion, chopped
2 Tbs. Miracle Whip, Light
2 Tbs. low-calorie yogurt
1 Tbs. wine vinegar
1 pkt. sweetener

Shred the cabbage. Cut sweet pickle, bell pepper, and onion in very small pieces. Make the dressing in another bowl, and mix all ingredients until well blended. Combine vegetable ingredients. Pour dressing over and mix well. It is best to cover the mixing bowl and set in the refrigerator for a couple of hours so that the flavors blend. If you have the time and inclination, you might want to crisp the cabbage by putting a few ice cubes over the shredded cabbage before mixing with other ingredients. If so, drain off water and ice before mixing.

4 Servings: 36.8 Calories per Serving; 1 gram Fat; 1.4 mg. Cholesterol, 0 Saturated Fat.

Food Exchanges: 0.7 vegetable; 0.4 fat.

———— Crunchy Cauliflower Salad ————

1 medium head cauliflower
1 cup sliced radishes
1/2 cup sliced green onions
1 8-oz. can sliced water chestnuts, drained*
1/4 cup Pet artificial sour cream
1/3 cup Miracle Whip, Light
2 tsp. caraway seeds
1 pkg. buttermilk dressing mix

Break cauliflower in flowerets. Combine cauliflower, radishes, green onions, and water chestnuts. Pour dressing of sour cream, mayonnaise or Miracle Whip, caraway seeds, and buttermilk dressing mix over vegetables and stir well. Spoon into salad bowl. Cover and chill before serving.

*Small slices of jicama may be substituted for the water chestnuts. The caloric difference is insignificant.

8 Servings: 61 Calories per Serving; 3 grams Fat; 1 mg. Cholesterol; 1.2 grams Saturated Fat.

Food Exchanges: 1 vegetable; 1 fat.

───── Cucumber and Onion Salad ─────

1/4 cup cold water
1/2 cup white vinegar
1 pkt. sweetener
2 tsp. dill weed
1 small onion, thinly sliced
1 medium cucumber, thinly sliced

Slice onions and cucumber. Mix water, vinegar, sweetener, and dill weed. Pour over onions and cucumber. Refrigerate until ready to serve. May be refrigerated overnight. This is very good with black-eyed peas.

4 Servings: 13 Calories per Serving; 0 Fat; 0 Cholesterol; 0 Saturated Fat.

Food Exchanges: 1/2 vegetable.

Try - could use Tuna or Turkey

───── Curried Chicken Salad ─────

1/4 cup Miracle Whip, Light
1/4 cup low-fat yogurt
1/2 tsp. lemon pepper
1-1/2 tsp. curry powder
1 Tbs. soy sauce, low sodium
1 cup celery, diced
1 can (15 oz.) pineapple chunks, unsweetened
1 can (8 oz.) water chestnuts
2 cups cooked chicken, diced
1/2 pkt. sweetener

In a bowl, mix mayonnaise, yogurt, lemon pepper, curry powder, and soy sauce. Add celery, pineapple, and water chestnuts. Add
chicken and mix thoroughly. Chill and serve.

*8 Servings: 139 Calories per Serving; 4 grams Fat; 39 mg.
Cholesterol; 0.5 grams Saturated Fat.*

Food Exchanges: 2 meats; 1/2 fruit.

Easy Aspic

My sister Lena made this (in larger quantity, of course)
for her book club in Dallas. When I recently visited a friend
in Western New York, she wanted to give me a great recipe
for aspic which she had just had at her book club. It turned
out to be the same recipe.

*1 3-oz. pkg. lemon Jello, sugar-free
2/3 cup boiling water
1 can (14-1/4 oz.) Hunt's stewed tomatoes*

Dissolve Jello in boiling water. Cut up the stewed tomatoes
and add. Pour into a 9x9" square casserole or baking pan and
refrigerate to set.

*9 Servings: 16 Calories per Serving; 0 Fat; 0 Cholesterol;
0.3 grams Saturated Fat.*

Food Exchanges: 1/2 vegetable.

English Pea Salad

This is the recipe which I remember from my childhood.
My mother made it with fresh English peas right out of her
garden, cooked of course. You and I will probably have to settle

Iny

for canned or frozen peas. We always used the term "English peas" because the word "peas" alone was used for black-eyed or cream peas.

> *2 cups cooked English peas, canned, frozen, or*
>   *fresh*
> *1/2 cup pimiento*
> *1/2 cup grated cheese, low fat*
> *2 Tbs. Miracle Whip, Light*
> *Salt and pepper*
> *Paprika*

In a saucepan, heat peas and pimiento. Add grated cheese and mayonnaise, and stir until cheese is melted. Add salt and pepper, and sprinkle paprika on top.

Serve warm or cold.

6 Servings: 81 Calories per Serving; 4 grams Fat; 8 mg. Cholesterol; 1.1 grams Saturated Fat.

Food Exchanges: 1 bread; 1 fat.

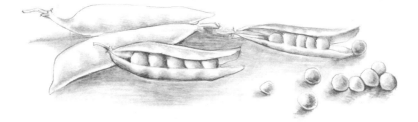

Try

—— Extra Crisp Red Cabbage Salad ——

1 medium-size red cabbage (about 2 lbs.)
1/2 cup red onion, chopped
15 ice cubes
1/2 cup red wine vinegar
1/4 cup water
2 Tbs. olive oil, or vegetable oil
1/2 tsp. salt
1 tsp. sugar
1 pkt. sweetener
1/8 tsp. pepper

Shred the cabbage in inch-long pieces. Chop the onion accordingly. Place one third of the cabbage and onion in bottom of a large bowl that can be covered tightly like a Tupperware bowl. Place 5 of the ice cubes on the cabbage and onions. Repeat the layers, ending with ice on top. Cover tightly and refrigerate several hours or overnight. Before serving, remove the remaining ice and drain all liquid from the bowl.

Combine vinegar, water, oil, salt, sugar, sweetener, and pepper in a screw-top jar. Shake well until blended. Pour over cabbage and toss. Makes about five cups.

10 Servings: 55 Calories per Serving; 3 grams Fat; 0 Cholesterol; 0.8 grams Saturated Fat.

Food Exchanges: 1/2 vegetable; 1/4 Fat.

Fall Fruit Chutney

1 cup cooked pumpkin, cubed
1/2 cup orange juice
1/4 cup brown sugar
1 tsp. Sweet'n Low
1 Tbs. lemon juice
1/4 tsp. ground ginger
1 three-inch stick cinnamon
2 medium apples, preferably tart
1/4 cup raisins

Peel a small cooking pumpkin (the large Halloween pumpkins make good jack-o'lanterns, but not much else). Scrape the seeds out and cut meat into 3/4-inch cubes. Place in a saucepan and cover with water. Cook just until tender but not mushy. Drain.

Combine orange juice, brown sugar, sweetener, lemon juice, ginger, and cinnamon together in a saucepan. Stir in cubed apples and cook on medium heat until apple is tender—about 7 minutes. Add pumpkin and raisins, and cook for 7 more minutes. This will keep in the refrigerator for several days.

This chutney adds sparkle to a fall or winter meal. The calories are calculated on 1/4-cup servings, but I use about half that much as a relish.

12 Servings: 45 Calories per Serving; 0 Fat; 0 Cholesterol; 0 Saturated Fat.

Food Exchanges: 1 fruit.

Ivy

——— Fresh Spinach Salad Supreme ———

6 fresh mushrooms, sliced
1/2 cup radishes, sliced
1 tsp. margarine
1 lb. fresh spinach
1/2 cup green onions, sliced
1/2 cup water chestnuts, or jicama, thinly sliced
1 Tbs. olive oil, or vegetable oil
2 Tbs. red wine vinegar
1 Tbs. lemon juice
1 pkt. sweetener
1/4 tsp. salt
1/2 tsp. lemon pepper
2 hard-boiled eggs, whites only
1 Tbs. bacon bits (imitation)

Sauté mushrooms in nonstick skillet with one teaspoon of margarine. If you use jicama instead of water chestnuts, sauté jicama slices with the mushrooms. Set aside. Combine spinach and onions in a large bowl and toss well. Combine olive oil, vinegar, lemon juice, sweetener, salt, and lemon pepper. Mix well. Add the dressing, mushrooms, and water chestnuts or jicama to spinach mixture. Toss gently. Sprinkle salad with sliced boiled egg whites and bacon bits. Toss the egg yolks down the garbage disposal.

8 Servings: 9 Calories per Serving; 0 Fat; 0 Cholesterol; 0 Saturated Fat.

Food Exchanges: Free.

Ivy

Grapefruit-Spinach Salad

This is one scrumptious dinner party salad, and so full of vitamins that you'll feel like dancing.

> 2 Tbs. vegetable oil
> 3 Tbs. grapefruit juice
> 2 Tbs. wine vinegar
> 1 Tbs. soy sauce (lite)
> 1/8 tsp. Tabasco sauce
> 1 pkg. fresh spinach
> 3 large grapefruit, peeled and sectioned
> 3 large oranges, peeled and sectioned
> 1 can (6 oz.) water chestnuts
> 1/4 lb. fresh mushrooms, sliced
> 2 Tbs. bacon bits (imitation)

Wash spinach, dry, break into bite-size pieces. Arrange bed of spinach in large salad bowl. Arrange grapefruit and oranges and water chestnuts over spinach. Pour dressing over spinach and fruit mixture. Chill. To serve, add mushrooms and bacon bits.

12 Servings: 96 Calories; 3 grams Fat; 0 Cholesterol; 0.4 grams Saturated Fat.

Food Exchanges: 1 fruit; 1 vegetable; 1/2 fat.

—— Green Grape and Onion Salad ——

1 large onion, preferably sweet
1/4 tsp. salt
1 cup water
6 ice cubes
2 pkts. sweetener
1/2 medium head lettuce
2-1/2 cups seedless grapes
1/2 tsp. curry powder
3 Tbs. Miracle Whip, Light
1 Tbs. lemon juice

Cut onion in half lengthwise. Then cut into thin slices. Combine water, ice cubes, and sweetener. Add onion slices and soak for one hour. Drain well.

Tear crisp lettuce into bite-size pieces. Cut the grapes in halves, lengthwise. Combine lettuce, onion, and 1-1/2 cups of grapes. Combine curry powder, lemon juice, and mayonnaise; add to lettuce mixture and toss gently. Garnish with the remaining grapes.

7 Servings: 62 Calories per Serving; 2 grams Fat; 2 mg. Cholesterol; 0.5 grams Saturated Fat.

Food Exchanges: 1/2 fruit; 1 vegetable.

Try

—— Holiday Cranberry Salad ——

1 lb. cranberries, chopped
1 can (10 oz.) mandarin oranges, drained
1 can (8 oz.) crushed pineapple, no sugar added, drained
2 tsp. sweetener
2 pkgs. (0.3 oz.) raspberry Jello, sugar-free

3/4 cup hot water
1-1/2 cups orange soda, sugar-free

Marinate cranberries, mandarin oranges, pineapple, and sweetener for at least an hour. Dissolve Jello in hot water. Add orange soda. When partially set, combine with fruit and pour into a 2-quart mold.

8 Servings: 51 Calories per Serving; 0 Fat; 0 Cholesterol; 0 Saturated Fat.

Food Exchanges: 1 fruit.

——— Jellied Vegetable Salad ———

1 pkg. (0.3 oz.) lemon or lime Jello, sugar-free
1/4 tsp. salt
1 cup boiling water
3/4 cup cold water
2 Tbs. apple vinegar
2 tsp. minced onion
Dash of pepper
3/4 cup cabbage, finely chopped
3/4 cup celery, finely chopped
1/2 cup radishes, finely sliced
2 Tbs. sliced pimiento
1/4 cup jicama, chopped (optional)

Dissolve Jello and salt in boiling water. Add cold water, vinegar, onion, and pepper. Chill until very thick, but not solid. Fold in vegetables. Pour into a one-quart mold or in 6 individual molds.

6 Servings: 16 Calories per Serving; 0 Fat; 0 Cholesterol; 0 Saturated Fat.

Food Exchanges: 1/2 vegetable.

—— Macaroni Cheddar Cheese Salad ——

1 Tbs. vegetable oil
1 Tbs. wine vinegar
1 Tbs. water
1 Tbs. Miracle Whip, Light
1/2 tsp. prepared mustard
1/2 tsp. Worcestershire sauce
1 pkt. sweetener
Salt and pepper to taste
1-1/3 cups cooked elbow macaroni
2 oz. (1/2 cup) Cheddar cheese, reduced fat,
   grated
2 Tbs. onion, chopped fine
2 Tbs. pimiento, chopped
2 Tbs. green pepper, chopped fine

Combine first seven ingredients in a salad bowl. Mix until smooth. Add cooked macaroni, onion, pimiento, green pepper, and salt and pepper. Mix thoroughly. May be served on lettuce, or garnished with parsley.

4 Servings: 121 Calories per Serving; .3 grams Fat; 0 Cholesterol; 1.7 grams Saturated Fat.

Food Exchanges: 1 bread; 1 fat.

Try

────────── Tuna Fish Salad ──────────

1 (6-1/2 oz.) can light tuna, water-packed
1 medium apple
1 boiled egg (discard the yolk)
1 pickle, small gherkin
1 tsp. chopped onion
1/2 cup celery, finely chopped
1/4 cup jicama, chopped 1/4" cubes (optional)
1/2 pkt. sugar substitute
1/4 tsp. lemon pepper
1/4 tsp. sweet basil
2 Tbs. Miracle Whip, Light

Mix all ingredients together until they are well blended. It is better if stored in refrigerator for a couple of hours for all flavors to blend. However, if you find yourself with nothing to serve and tempted to call the pizza man, make the salad and serve immediately. Nip that craving for store-bought pizza in the bud—fill up on Tuna Fish Salad. This can be served on a bed of lettuce, surrounded by carrot sticks and tomatoes. If you crave something a bit more filling, spread the tuna salad between 2 slices of 40-calorie bread.

4 Servings: 98 Calories per Serving; 1 gram Fat; 2 mg. Cholesterol; 0 Saturated Fat.

Food Exchanges: 1-1/2 meat; 1 fat; 1/2 fruit.

Marinated Cucumber Salad

2 medium cucumbers, thinly sliced
1 medium onion, in rings
1/2 cup carrots, thinly sliced
1/2 cup celery, chopped
1 cup vinegar
2 Tbs. vegetable oil
2 tsp. Sweet'n Low
1 tsp. celery seed
1 tsp. salt
1/2 tsp. pepper
Leaf lettuce, about 6 leaves to line salad bowl

Combine cucumber, onion, carrots, and celery in large bowl. Set aside. Combine vinegar, oil, sweetener, celery seed, salt and pepper. Pour over vegetables and toss gently. Cover the bowl tightly and chill for ten hours.

When ready to serve, drain liquid off and serve in a lettuce-lined salad bowl.

8 Servings: 53 Calories per Serving; 4 grams Fat; 0 Cholesterol; 0 Saturated Fat.

Food Exchanges: 1 vegetable; 1/2 fat.

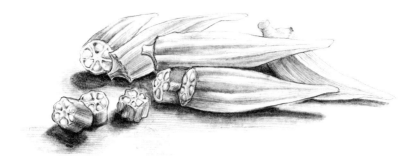

Okra Salad

1 lb. okra
3 tomatoes
1 medium onion
Salt to taste
Black pepper
1/4 cup cornmeal
1 Tbs. vegetable cooking oil

Cut okra into bite-size pieces. Sprinkle with salt and pepper and dredge in cornmeal.

Pan fry in Teflon skillet with 1 Tbs. vegetable cooking oil. While okra is frying, chop tomatoes and onions. When okra is tender and light brown, mix with tomatoes and onion. Seal in covered bowl. Let set a few minutes before serving.

I got this recipe from my sister Jennie who says that this is a popular dish at the potluck suppers at her church.

8 Servings: 64 Calories per Serving; 2 grams Fat; 0 Cholesterol; 0.3 grams Saturated Fat.

Food Exchanges: 1 vegetable; 1/2 bread.

Try

—————————— **Salmon Salad** ——————————

1 can (15 oz.) salmon
2 Tbs. minced green onions with tops
2 Tbs. celery, chopped
1 Tbs. vegetable oil
1-1/2 Tbs. lemon juice
1 clove garlic, minced
1/8 tsp. dry mustard
1/4 tsp. salt
1/2 tsp. sweet basil
Dash of paprika
1 tomato
Parsley

Toss salmon with green onions and celery lightly, keeping salmon in chunks. Combine remaining ingredients, except tomato and parsley, and blend thoroughly. Pour over salmon mixture. Garnish with tomato and parsley.

6 Servings: 130 Calories per Serving; 7 grams Fat; 0 Cholesterol; 1 gram Saturated Fat.

Food Exchanges: 2 meat; 1/2 fat.

—————————— **Sauerkraut Salad** ——————————

2 cups chopped sauerkraut, drained
2 Tbs. sugar
1 tsp. Sweet'n Low
1/2 cup celery, thinly sliced
1/2 cup bell pepper, chopped
1/2 cup carrots, grated

1/2 cup onion, chopped
1 jar (2 oz.) pimiento, drained

Combine sauerkraut, sugar, and sweetener. Let stand for thirty minutes. Add remaining ingredients and stir well. Cover and refrigerate for at least twelve hours.

8 Servings: 34 Calories per Serving; 0 Fat; 0 Cholesterol; 0 Saturated Fat.

Food Exchanges: 1 vegetable.

———— Shrimp Salad ————

This is the first time that I have put this recipe in writing after all those years of serving shrimp when I lived on South Padre Island, Texas. That was where we were assured that the shrimp we bought had slept in the Gulf the night before. My sister called me long distance after returning home to Dallas from visiting me on the Island. She desperately wanted my recipe for Shrimp Salad. I could not give it to her. In the first place, I had never measured ingredients. In the second place, I couldn't remember precisely what those ingredients were.

Lena, this is the recipe you asked for. Sorry it is ten years late in getting to you.

1 lb. shrimp, uncooked in shells (makes 2 cups cooked and chopped)
1/4 tsp. salt
2 boiled eggs (use only whites)
1/2 cup celery, chopped
2 sweet gherkins, 2-inch

1/2 pkt. sweetener
1/4 cup pimientos
1 Tbs. capers (optional)
1 tsp. Worcestershire sauce
1/4 tsp. Tabasco sauce
3 Tbs. Miracle Whip, Light
1/2 tsp. paprika
1/2 tsp. salt
1 tsp. wine vinegar
1/2 tsp. lemon pepper

Select fresh or quick-frozen shrimp. I prefer fresh but will accept frozen. I do not want previously frozen shrimp that has already been thawed before I get it. If shrimp is frozen, pour warm water over it and break up the block somewhat before putting it in boiling water so that shrimp will cook evenly. Otherwise, the outside shrimp will be mushy before the inside ones are done.

Put 4 quarts of water in a large pot. Add 1/4 tsp. salt. Bring to a rolling boil. Add shrimp. When water returns to a rolling boil, time it and let boil for 3 minutes, or until shells turn pink. Do not overcook. Drain off water and dump shrimp into a pan of ice cubes. Be sure that each shrimp touches the ice. Let set until shrimp is cool enough to peel. Don't peel them until ready to use. If I need to store them in refrigerator for a while, I put more ice over them and cover the bowl. When peeling the shrimp, cut out the thin black line on the top, then put back on ice.

Cut the shrimp crosswise into 1/4″ pieces. Add chopped celery and chopped egg whites; then pickle, pimiento, and capers. Mix Worcestershire sauce, mayonnaise, mustard, sweetener, and Tabasco sauce together, blending well. Fold mayonnaise mixture into the shrimp. Sprinkle paprika and white pepper on top. If possible, prepare three or four hours ahead of time so that flavors blend. Cover with saran wrap and place in refrigerator.

Combine all vegetables. Mix vinegar, oil, sugar, sugar substitute, salt, and pepper, and pour over vegetables. Toss until well mixed. If desired, top with thinly sliced bell pepper and thinly sliced onions in addition to those in the salad. Refrigerate for at least five hours or overnight. Will keep in the refrigerator several days.

12 Servings: 91 Calories per Serving; 0.1 grams Fat; 0 Cholesterol; 0.6 grams Saturated Fat.

Food Exchanges: 1/2 bread; 1 fat.

—— Tossed Salad with Grapefruit ——

> 2 cups lettuce, torn into pieces
> 2 green onions
> 1/4 of a bell pepper
> 1/2 medium zucchini
> 6 thin slices cucumber
> 1 grapefruit
> 1/4 cup jicama cubes
> 1 garlic bud
> 1 Tbs. grated Parmesan cheese
> 2 Tbs. Kraft or Wishbone Lite Italian Dressing
>   (6 cal. per Tbs.)

Crisp lettuce in advance. You may use leaf lettuce or head lettuce, or both. Tear the lettuce into bite-size pieces. Tearing is preferable to cutting.

Peel grapefruit and divide into segments. See page 186 in Fruit Section of Desserts chapter.

Cut up onions, zucchini, jicama, bell pepper, and garlic. Gently toss lettuce, grapefruit, and vegetables together. Add two tablespoons of salad dressing, and toss gently. Sprinkle one tablespoon of grated Parmesan cheese on top. This is a basic tossed green salad. In the summertime, you can substitute tomatoes or cantaloupe for the grapefruit. You can also add radishes, and many other raw vegetables.

3 Servings: 43 Calories per Serving; 0.8 grams Fat; 1.6 mg. Cholesterol; 0 Saturated Fat.

Food Exchanges: 2/3 vegetable; 1 fruit; 1/3 meat.

Waldorf Salad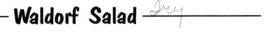

4 medium apples, good eating kind
2 cups celery, chopped
1/2 tsp. black walnut extract
1/4 cup Miracle Whip, Light

Wash, core, and dice apples into 1/2-inch cubes. Do not peel. Add apple cubes to chopped celery. Mix walnut extract with mayonnaise. Blend mayonnaise with celery and apple mixture.

According to a story in *Heloise*, the original Waldorf Salad contained only apples, celery, and mayonnaise. Through the years, cooks have added raisins, nuts, and whatever. We will keep ours "light" by adding the black walnut extract and low-fat mayo.

6 Servings: 75 Calories per Serving; 2.5 grams Fat; 3.5 mg. Cholesterol; .08 grams Saturated Fat.

Food Exchanges: 1 fruit; 1/2 vegetable; 3/4 fat.

Wilted Lettuce

1/2 a large bunch of leaf lettuce
3 green onions, chopped, including the green blades
6 radishes, sliced
1 boiled egg (discard yolk)
2 tsp. vegetable oil
2 Tbs. red wine vinegar

2 Tbs. water
Pepper and salt

Tear lettuce into large bite-size pieces. Add onions and radishes. Heat oil, vinegar, and water in a skillet. Toss in greens and stir until slightly wilted—about one minute. Add salt, pepper, and sliced white of boiled egg.

4 Servings: 32 Calories per Serving; 2-1/4 grams Fat; 0 Cholesterol; 0.4 grams Saturated Fat.

Food Exchanges: 1-1/2 vegetable.

Wilted Spinach

1 bag (10 oz.) fresh spinach
1/2 cup green onions, chopped
1/2 cup radishes, chopped
2 Tbs. bacon bits (imitation)
1 Tbs. vegetable oil
1/4 cup cider vinegar
1 pkt. sugar substitute
1/4 tsp. salt
1/4 tsp. pepper

Rinse and drain spinach. Tear into bite-size pieces. Combine spinach, onions, and radishes in large bowl. Sprinkle imitation bacon bits on top, and set aside.

In a small skillet, add vinegar, vegetable oil, sweetener, salt, and pepper. Heat to bubbling. Pour over the salad and toss gently. Serve immediately.

4 Servings: 62 Calories per Serving; 4 grams Fat; 0 Cholesterol; 0.5 grams Saturated Fat.

Food Exchanges: 1 vegetable; 1 fat.

Entrées

ENTREES

In *Mrs. Blackwell's* I told you how to wring a chicken's neck, and how to cut up a chicken into sixteen pieces. I also told you about hog-killing time. I did not tell you much about fishing—unless the account of our frog gigging would qualify as fishing. Nowadays, you don't have time to raise chickens and hogs and help with the butchering and "putting up" the meat. Leave that up to Holly Farms, Armour and Co., Swift, Texas' own Bo Pilgrim, and others. You have more important things to do—like walking, jogging, or running, like riding your bicycle, stationary or otherwise, or going to aerobics or swimming classes.

This is the modern way to select your chicken, or fish, or meat: Run, walk, or bicycle down to your favorite supermarket; if the distance is over a mile or two, drive your car if you must. Park your car on the far side of the parking lot. Walk briskly up to the self-opening doors. Get a cart and head straight for the poultry counters. Look neither to the right nor to the left . . . on one side, right up front, you would see an aisle counter piled high with pudding or rum cakes—if you looked. And on the other side you would see an upright counter filled with potato chips, Fritos, or George Bush's pork rinds poised to leap into your basket if you get too close. After you are safely beyond these tempting snacks, there is the frozen yogurt machine beckoning you to squirt your own yogurt into the handy cups nearby. And you could select your own topping, any one of which would blow your balanced food program for a week. You could be tempted to eat your frozen yogurt in the store and throw away the cup, thus escaping the telltale sign left in your car like a candy wrapper or a doughnut paper. Just walk on by! Take the cleaning products or automotive aisle to the back of the store. Go directly to the poultry section of the meat counter.

At the poultry counter, you are faced with many decisions. You might want to limit your selection to chicken breasts. You can buy chicken filets which have been deboned, skinned, and defatted. These look very expensive by the pound, but probably are no more expensive than the split breast by the time you do your own skinning, deboning, and defatting. If you opt for the split breasts, promise me that you will take the skin off and cut away every speck of that ugly yellow chicken fat before you put it in the freezer or the pot.

Stay away from the chicken wings that are so popular nowadays for barbecuing or deep frying. Chicken wings are mostly skin, fat, and bones. You can't eat the bones, and you shouldn't eat the skin and fat. If you were born into a large family like I was, the wing or the neck was the only piece of chicken you ever got to eat. You are entitled to a better piece now. When my daughter, the third child, came along, I cut the tip off one of the wings and told her it was a special pulley bone. Her two older brothers already had dibs on the two pulley bones. After all, I couldn't fry three chickens for dinner every Sunday so that my kids would not fight over the pulley bones. The wing is still my daughter's favorite piece. I must talk to her about that.

I'm afraid someone hoodwinked the American public, like I did my little girl, into thinking that chicken wings are a special delicacy.

After you have selected your chicken, proceed to the fish counter. There are several different fish which you might select. You might want to choose orange roughy, that lovely white-meated fish from New Zealand without a fishy smell. If it is available, there is nothing better than red snapper or redfish from the Texas Gulf. Catfish is very plentiful where I live, but I find it a little fatty. It is great for deep frying, but of course we are not going to be doing any deep-fat frying. You might choose shrimp to boil, crabmeat, or oysters unless you are on a severely restricted no-cholesterol diet.

When you come to the red-meat counter, pick tenderloin or sirloin as they have less concentration of fat. Buy only lean ground meat. Ground round is all right, but stay away from ground chuck or regular hamburger meat.

Move on down to the frozen food counter and pick up a package of ground turkey. You might also want to buy some turkey sausage, and occasionally you should buy a turkey breast . . . it is often a good buy, and it is lower in calories than chicken. Personally, I'm so old-fashioned that I never think about roast turkey except at Thanksgiving and Christmastime.

After you have selected your fresh and frozen meat, stop by the canned meat section and pick up a couple of cans of chunk light tuna packed in spring water—or just water. It is a good idea to keep a supply of tuna on hand at all times so you will have it when you need to prepare a quick low-calorie meal.

No need to go by the dairy counter, bread shelf, or produce section. We'll get to them in later chapters.

I have given you only a few meat recipes. You already know that broiling or baking meat is the preferable way to cook it. I hope you have developed the habit of cutting off all visible fat before cooking.

Wild Rice—The Original American Staple

Unless you have lived on or around one of Minnesota's ten thousand lakes, you probably never considered wild rice as country-cooking fare. Wild rice was a staple food of woodland Indians and only became a gourmet food in the twentieth century. When my children were about the right age to enjoy family outings and family fishing trips, we lived in Minneapolis for seventeen wonderful months, including two summers.

Each summer we spent a couple of weeks on Leech Lake, a hundred or so miles north of Minneapolis—and, incidentally, the wild rice capital of the country. It was there that we fell in love with wild rice and the many tales surrounding it. We fished for the spirited great northern pike, and the evasive walleye, being careful not to get our outboard motor tangled in the coarse blades of wild rice growing profusely in the lake. We were never there during the harvest time, the reason being that the cabins were booked up from one year to the next by the native city folks who went there to harvest wild rice.

The story was that only native Americans, as in American Indians, were permitted to harvest wild rice on the ten thousand lakes of Minnesota. The locals around Leech Lake told us that during wild rice harvesting time, the city doctors, lawyers, and businessmen in the Twin Cities suddenly became American Indians and flocked to Leech Lake for wild rice harvesting. The method of harvesting was very primitive: one person steered the small canoe while the second person beat the grain off the stalk into the bottom of the boat.

After moving from Minneapolis in 1960, I always managed to buy a teeny package of wild rice about once a year. It was like buying pure gold. Stores in the Washington D.C. area kept the boxes of wild rice under the cash register

Several years later we moved from Washington to South Padre Island, off the Texas Coast. There, a longtime friend of mine complained to me that our mutual friend, Cil Webb, who then lived in Northern Minnesota, sent her the "dumbest Christmas present." For years Cil had sent Betty a Hummel Christmas plate, and this year she sent her a box of rice, of all things. My ears pricked up at the thought of rice from Minnesota. It *had* to be wild rice. I asked to see it. Sure enough, it was a five-pound package of wild rice. The very idea of five pounds of pure wild rice, not a box of brown or white rice with a few gains of wild sprinkled in, sent my heart racing and my mouth salivating. I explained to my friend that she had received a veritable bonanza, and I unselfishly promised to show her how to cook it, fully expecting her to share her bounty with me. My friend Betty, God rest her soul, died suddenly a couple of weeks later, and I inherited, not a valuable collection of Hummel Christmas plates, but five pounds of Minnesota wild rice.

In thinking about this story, I began to wonder if modern technology had not taken over the growing and harvesting of wild rice, especially since it does not seem so rare these days. I contacted the Visitors' Information Center of Leech Lake, Minnesota. Horror of horrors, my suspicions were confirmed. "Wild rice" is now being cultivated in rice paddies in California and elsewhere with the use of herbicides and fertilizers, and hauled halfway across the continent to Minnesota processing plants for roasting, threshing, fanning, and packaging. Those who know wild rice say they can tell the difference between the real thing and the commercial paddy rice. They say the new stuff is black instead of dark brown and that the taste is different. The Minnesota legislature is considering labeling laws which would prohibit the domesticated product being called "Wild Rice."

There is another story connected with my wild rice bonanza. With five pounds of the stuff, I was fairly generous in serving it to guests. I gave a dinner party for ten people and served Rock Cornish hens and wild rice. The table was set to perfection and the game hens and wild rice cooked to a turn. The guests had finished their cocktails and were finding their places at the table. I was in the kitchen heating up the mushroom gravy immediately prior to serving. I took from the refrigerator a fruit jar which I thought contained cooking wine, and dumped it into the gravy pan. Two big lumps fell into the pan. It was not red wine in the fruit jar but pickled beet juice along with two pieces of beets, and I had dumped it into the mushroom gravy to be served over the wild rice! As the guests were taking their seats at the table, my mushroom gravy was turning a deep purplish grey. Frantically, I stirred beef bouillon into the gray to disguise the color, and white wine to disguise the pickled-beet taste. The guests raved about the gourmet dinner. Only the hostess was the wiser.

CHICKEN

Rock Cornish Hens

3 Rock Cornish hens
1 Tbs. low-fat margarine
Salt and pepper

Split Cornish hens in half by cutting down the middle of breast and back bone. Wash and pat dry. Lightly salt and pepper the halves. Place halves cut side down in a roasting pan which has been coated with vegetable cooking spray. Lightly rub margarine over pieces. Cover lightly with foil wrap. Roast in moderate oven (350°) for about 40 minutes. Remove foil and bake 20 more minutes. When hens are tender, transfer to a casserole baking dish, with split side up. Spoon about 1/2 cup of wild rice stuffing onto each half. Brown in oven for 10 or 15 minutes. Serve immediately with mushroom gravy.

4 Servings: 150 Calories per Serving; 10 grams Fat; 30 mg. Cholesterol; 0.8 grams Saturated Fat.

Food Exchanges: 2 meats; 1 fat.

Wild Rice Stuffing

1/2 cup wild rice, uncooked
2 cups chicken broth, homemade, with fat
   skimmed off
1/2 cup celery, chopped
1/4 cup onion, minced
1/2 cup mushrooms, sliced, either fresh or canned
1 oz. dry white wine
1/2 tsp. thyme
1/2 tsp. sweet basil

1/4 tsp. salt
1/4 tsp. pepper or lemon pepper

Wash rice very carefully. Bring chicken broth to a boil and add wild rice. Reduce heat to medium and cook for 40 minutes. In the meantime, sauté celery, onions, and mushrooms in a large skillet sprayed with vegetable cooking spray. Add rice and all other ingredients to the large skillet. Cover tightly and cook on low heat for about 30 minutes. Use as stuffing for Rock Cornish hens, or as a side dish with chicken, turkey, fish, or beef.

6 Servings: 98 Calories per Serving; 2 grams Fat; 0 Cholesterol; 0 Saturated Fat.

Food Exchanges: 1 bread.

Mushroom Gravy

1 Tbs. low-fat margarine
2 Tbs. flour
1 cup sliced mushrooms
1-1/2 cups chicken broth
Salt and pepper
1 oz. white wine

Melt margarine in nonstick skillet. Sauté mushrooms until light golden in color. Add flour, salt and pepper, and mix well. Gradually add chicken broth and white wine. Continue stirring. Cook until slightly thickened and bubbly.

6 Servings: 34 Calories per Serving; 3 grams Fat; 0.5 mg. Cholesterol; 0.6 grams Saturated Fat.

Food Exchanges: 1/2 bread.

Try

—— Wild Rice Chicken Casserole ——

4 oz. wild rice, uncooked
2 cups water
1 Tbs. low-fat margarine
3 Tbs. flour
1 cup chicken broth, homemade, with fat skimmed
  off
1-1/2 cups canned skim milk
1/4 tsp. salt
2 cups boiled chicken, diced, breasts with no skin
1/4 cup mushrooms, sliced
1/4 cup pimiento, chopped
1/3 cup bell pepper, chopped
1/4 cup water chestnuts, sliced

Wash rice very carefully. Bring water to a boil; add rice; reduce heat to medium and cook covered for about 40 minutes.

To make a flour paste, put flour and one cup of milk in a pint jar. Put lid on and shake until flour is completely mixed.

Melt margarine in a skillet. Sauté chopped bell pepper; then transfer to another bowl. Pour flour paste, broth, and remaining milk into the skillet. Mix until smooth. Cook this sauce until thickened, stirring constantly.

Mix together cooked wild rice, chicken, mushrooms, pimientos, sautéed bell peppers and water chestnuts. Pour into a Pam-sprayed baking dish (6x10"). Pour sauce over all. Bake in moderate oven (350°) for 40 minutes.

8 Servings: 244 Calories per Serving; 3 grams Fat; 50 mg. Cholesterol; 1 gram Saturated Fat.

Food Exchanges: 2 meat; 1 bread; 1/2 skimmed milk.

Chicken Stock

One 4-lb. chicken, skin and fat removed
8 cups cold water
1 carrot, sliced
2 celery stalks
1/2 bay leaf
3 whole black peppers or 1/4 tsp. ground black
  pepper
1 onion, sliced
1/4 tsp. salt

After you have skinned the chicken, cut it in pieces and remove all visible fat. Put all pieces, except breast, in pot with cold water. Add vegetables and seasoning. Bring to boil. Add breasts. Simmer until breast is tender. Take chicken pieces out of the broth. Chicken may be used for casseroles or salad.

Pour broth into a container and place in the refrigerator. Let cool for several hours until all fat has risen to the top. Skim off fat. Chicken broth is rather fragile and should not be kept in refrigerator more than a couple of days. I pour it into small freezer containers or margarine cups and freeze. It is a good idea to have chicken broth on hand at all times for use in cooking vegetables, soups, and as broth for casseroles. You may use low-sodium canned chicken broth, but I prefer the homemade kind.

It was not possible to calculate the calorie and food count of this with our computer program. Kathy used the calorie count for chicken broth given in the program, which was as follows:

1 Cup: 39 Calories; 1.39 grams Fat; 1 mg. Cholesterol; 0.4 grams Saturated Fat.

Food Exchanges: 2/3 meat.

– Baked Chicken with Buttermilk Sauce –

One 3-lb. frying chicken
3/4 cup water
1 Tbs. instant chicken bouillon granules
1/2 tsp. sweet basil
1/2 tsp. dried rosemary
2 bay leaves
4 medium red potatoes
3 carrots
2 medium onions
1/2 cup low-fat buttermilk
3 Tbs. flour
Paprika
Salt
Pepper

Cut up chicken into serving pieces. Remove the skin and all visible fat. Brown chicken pieces in nonstick skillet which has been coated with vegetable cooking spray. Place chicken pieces in sprayed casserole baking dish. Wash and quarter the red potatoes, leaving skin on. Peel carrots and cut into one-inch pieces. Cut onion in vertical slices. Arrange potatoes, carrots, and onions around chicken pieces. Sprinkle sweet basil and rosemary on chicken. Pour 3/4 cup of water over chicken and vegetables. Add bay leaves. Cover lightly with foil and bake in preheated 350° oven for 45 minutes to one hour, until chicken is tender. Take off foil the last 15 minutes for chicken to brown evenly.

Transfer chicken and vegetables to serving platter and keep warm. Pour juices out of casserole into a skillet and add water to make a cup of liquid. Combine buttermilk and flour and add to liquid in the skillet, stirring constantly to blend. Cook on medium heat for five minutes or so until you have a thickened, bubbly gravy. In the meantime, sprinkle paprika over chicken. Pour gravy over chicken, or place in gravy bowl and pass around. Who says you can't have cream gravy while watching your calories?

8 Servings: 115 Calories per Serving; 5 grams Fat; 45 mg. Cholesterol; 1 gram Saturated Fat.

Food Exchanges: 2 meat.

Try

Baked Chicken in a Bag

4 chicken breasts or thighs
1 garlic clove
1/2 tsp. sweet basil
1/2 tsp. salt
1/2 tsp. pepper
1 tsp. paprika

Remove skin and all visible signs of fat from the chicken. Sprinkle on salt, pepper, sweet basil, and paprika. Mince the garlic and place some on each piece. Place chicken pieces in a baking bag. (Do not make the mistake that I once did in inadvertently using a Baggie. It was an unholy mess.) Be sure to follow instructions on the box. Bake in 350° oven for about 50 minutes, or until chicken turns a golden brown.

Save the natural gravy. Pour into a bowl and place in refrigerator. As it cools, any grease will rise to the top; skim it off and save to season something else later.

If you have honestly skinned the chicken and cut away all the fat, you may add quartered potatoes, whole carrots, and a medium-size onion. Then you will have a complete meal in a bag.

4 Servings:

Chicken breasts: *167 Calories per Serving; 4 grams Fat; 84 mg. Cholesterol; 1 gram Saturated Fat.*

Food Exchanges: 3 meat; 0 fat.

Chicken thighs: *112 Calories per Serving; 6 grams Fat; 49 mg. Cholesterol; 2 grams Saturated Fat.*

Food Exchanges: 2 meat; 0 fat.

———— Chicken with Almonds ————

> 1 tsp. low-fat margarine
> 1/4 cup chopped almonds
> 2 tsp. curry powder, divided
> 1 cup apple, diced unpeeled
> 1/2 cup onion, chopped
> 1/2 cup fresh mushrooms, sliced
> 1 Tbs. flour
> 1 tsp. chicken-flavored bouillon
> 1 cup boiling water
> 1/2 cup skim milk
> 1 Tbs. lemon juice
> 1 cup cooked chicken breast, chopped

Melt margarine in a large skillet over medium heat. Add almonds. Cook for ten minutes, stirring frequently, or until almonds are slightly browned. Sprinkle one teaspoon of the curry powder over the almonds. Toss lightly to coat. Drain almonds on paper towel.

Place apple, onion, and mushrooms in the skillet and sauté for five minutes. Stir in remaining 1 teaspoon of the curry powder and flour. Cook over low heat 2 minutes, stirring frequently.

Dissolve bouillon in boiling water. Add to skillet with milk and lemon juice. Cook over low heat about 5 minutes or until smooth and thickened, stirring constantly. Add chicken. Continue to cook over low heat, stirring until thoroughly heated.

You're going to love this recipe!

5 Servings: 125 Calories per Serving; 5 grams Fat; 27 mg. Cholesterol; 0.9 grams Saturated Fat.

Food Exchanges: 1-1/2 meat; 1 fat.

You can serve this over 1/2 cup rice per serving. Add 80 calories per serving. No fat and no cholesterol. Add one bread exchange.

Easy, Fry

—————— Chicken Breasts Surprise ——————

6 chicken breast halves, boned and skinned
1 jar (2-1/2 oz.) dried beef
1 can (10-3/4 oz.) Weight Watchers cream of
*   mushroom soup*
1 jar (2-1/2 oz.) sliced mushrooms
1/2 tsp. parsley flakes
1/2 tsp. sweet basil
1/4 cup white wine or sherry, if desired

Lay dried beef slices on bottom of Pam-sprayed casserole baking dish. Place chicken breast halves on top of dried beef slices. Pour soup over chicken and scatter mushrooms on top.

Sprinkle parsley and rosemary on top. Cover and bake one and one-half hours. Remove cover and cook for 20 minutes more. The surprise is that no one expects or will be able to identify this combination of ingredients.

6 Servings: 185 Calories per Serving; 4 grams Fat; 83 mg. Cholesterol; 1 gram Saturated Fat.

Food Exchanges: 3 meat.

Dry

— Chicken Breasts in Cheese Sauce —

4 chicken breast halves
1 Tbs. low-fat margarine
2 Tbs. flour
2 cups skim milk
1/2 cup (2 oz.) shredded Swiss cheese
4 Tbs. Parmesan cheese, finely grated
2 cans (4 oz.) sliced mushrooms, drained
1/2 tsp. salt
Pepper
1/2 tsp. paprika

Skin chicken breasts and cut away all visible fat. Cook chicken by putting it in pot with 4 cups of water. Let come to a boil. Lower heat to medium and cook covered for 30 minutes or until completely tender. Take chicken off the bone and place back in broth to keep warm. Set aside but keep on low heat.

To make sauce, heat margarine in heavy saucepan over low heat. Add flour to 1/2 cup milk in jar with a lid. Shake the jar until flour is well blended. Add to remaining milk and gradually to margarine, stirring constantly until thickened. Add cheese, mushrooms, water chestnuts, salt and pepper. Cook until cheese melts and sauce is thoroughly heated.

Place chicken pieces in warmed platter and pour cheese sauce over them. Sprinkle with paprika and serve immediately.

6 Servings: 209 Calories per Serving; 9 grams Fat; 64 mg. Cholesterol; 6 grams Saturated Fat.

Food Exchanges: 2-2/3 meat; 2/3 fat; 1/2 milk.

Fry

————————— Chicken and Broccoli —————————

4 chicken breasts (14 oz. cooked and boned)
1 bunch fresh broccoli
1/4 cup low-fat margarine
1/4 cup flour
2 cups chicken broth (homemade after boiling the
*   chicken)*
1/4 cup canned evaporated skim milk
1/4 tsp. salt
3/4 cup grated cheese

Boil the chicken breasts in 3 cups of water. While chicken is boiling, steam broccoli in microwave if you have a microwave steamer, or cook broccoli in a pot on top of the stove. When broccoli is done, cut into 1/2-inch chunks. When chicken is tender, debone and cut into 1-inch slices.

Melt margarine in a Teflon skillet. Cream flour in margarine. Add chicken broth and canned skim milk, and cook while stirring until completely blended.

Spray a casserole pan with vegetable cooking spray. Place a layer of chicken in bottom; add onions and broccoli. Pour over half of the creamed broth. Sprinkle half of the cheese over mixture. Repeat the process, ending with cheese on top. Bake in 350° oven for 45 minutes.

8 Servings: 138 Calories per Serving; 5 grams Fat; 38 mg. Cholesterol; 1.4 grams Saturated Fat.

Food Exchanges: 2 meat; 1 vegetable; 1/2 fat.

Chicken Chow Mein

2 cups diced cooked chicken
1/2 lb. lean pork
1/2 lb. veal
6 Tbs. soy sauce, light
1 cup water
1 medium bunch of celery
1 small onion, chopped
2 Tbs. cornstarch
1/4 cup water
1 can (10-1/2 oz.) water chestnuts
1 can (#2) bean sprouts
1 can (2 oz.) mushrooms
Salt and pepper
4 cups cooked rice

Brown meats in skillet sprayed with vegetable cooking spray. Add chicken, soy sauce, and 1 cup of water. Simmer 2 minutes. Add celery and onions, simmer 1-1/2 hours. Blend cornstarch and water. Stir into meat mixture. Add chestnuts, bean sprouts, and mushrooms. Add seasoning, and simmer until well blended and heated through. Serve over cooked rice. Allow 1/2 cup rice per serving.

8 Servings: 293 Calories per Serving; 9 grams Fat; 62 mg. Cholesterol; 2 grams Saturated Fat.

Food Exchanges: 3 meat; 1 vegetable; 1 bread.

Dry

Chicken and Dumplings

> 1 whole chicken, or 4 split breasts
> 1/2 tsp. salt
> 1/2 tsp. pepper
> 2 qts. water
> 2 chicken bouillon cubes
> 1/2 cup skim milk

add sliced carrots & celery

Skin the chicken and take off all visible fat. Cut the wings off and toss them, because they are nothing but fatty skin and bones. Cut the rest in smaller pieces, lightly salt and pepper, and place in a pot with 2 quarts of water. Boil for 45 minutes with a loose-fitting lid on the pot. (Chicken will boil over very easily, and you'll have a big mess to clean up.) When done, take out of pot and debone. While chicken is cooking, make the dumplings (see below).

Put chicken pieces back into the pot and bring to a brisk boil. Slowly add the dumpling pieces so that the brisk boil does not subside. When all pieces are in, lower the heat and cook for about thirty minutes. Add 1/2 cup skim milk immediately after dumplings are done.

Dumplings

> 1 egg, or 1/4 cup egg substitute
> 1 cup flour
> 1/4 tsp salt
> 1 Tbs. water

Slightly beat eggs and add water and salt. Slowly stir flour into egg mixture. This should be very stiff. Roll out on floured pastry board with a rolling pin—very thin, about 1/8-inch thick. Cut into strips one inch wide and four or five inches long.

Note: These are the Southern Illinois country dumplings. In that part of the country, they put them into many different things. Would you believe, stewed fresh corn, sauerkraut, boiled new potatoes, and beans? I like them in the corn, and the boiled new potatoes, but the sauerkraut, well . . .

6 Servings: 203 Calories per Serving; 1 gram Fat; 57 mg. Cholesterol; 1 gram Saturated Fat.

Food Exchanges: 2-1/2 meat; 1 bread; 1 fat.

Chicken á la King

Dry

    2 Tbs. low-fat margarine
    2 Tbs. Butter Buds (add liquid according to
      directions)
    1/4 cup flour
    1/4 tsp. salt
    1 cup skim milk
    1 cup low-fat yogurt
    1 cup chicken broth, homemade with fat skimmed
      from top
    4 chicken breast halves, cooked (1-1/2 cups
      bite-size cubes)
    1/3 cup mushrooms
    3 Tbs. pimiento, diced
    1/2 cup bell pepper, finely cut
    1/4 cup onions, finely chopped
    8 slices of white bread (light, 40 cal.)

Cook chicken breasts ahead of time by boiling in cooking pot with 4 cups of water. You may want to put a stem of celery in with the chicken. Save the stock and refrigerate for several hours, until all the fat has risen to the top. Skim off all the congealed fat. Cut the chicken into bite-size pieces.

Blend flour with 1/2 cup of milk in jar with lid. Shake until flour is blended. Melt margarine in large skillet. Add milk with flour, plus remaining milk, yogurt, and chicken stock to skillet. Cook thoroughly until thick. Add chicken breasts in bite-size cubes.

Sauté green pepper, mushrooms, and onion in small skillet coated with vegetable cooking spray. Stir in pimiento and add all vegetables to chicken mixture. Heat the total mixture until bubbly.

Immediately before serving, cut slices of bread in half and toast them. Spoon hot Chicken á la King over toasted bread.

8 Servings: 193 Calories; 5 grams Fat; 48 mg. Cholesterol; 1 gram Saturated Fat.

Food Exchanges: 2 meat; 1 bread; 1/2 fat.

Chicken Supreme

4 chicken breast halves
1/2 tsp. pepper
1 Tbs. margarine
1 tsp. Mrs. Dash
1/4 tsp. paprika
1 medium onion, thinly sliced
1 cup mushrooms, sliced

Cut up chicken. Skin and take off all visible fat. Sprinkle with pepper, Mrs. Dash, and paprika. Melt margarine in Teflon skillet. Brown chicken on both sides, then cook slowly for about 30 minutes. Remove chicken and keep hot. In the same pan, sauté onions and mushrooms until translucent. Place chicken back in the skillet and spread the onions and mushrooms over it. Cover and continue cooking at 300° until chicken is tender—about 30 minutes.

6 Servings: 247 Calories per Serving; 13 grams Fat; 96 mg. Cholesterol; 3.4 grams Saturated Fat.

Food Exchanges: 4 meat; 1 fat.

Chicken Curry Crepes

Basic Crepe Recipe

I cup flour
1/2 cup skim milk
1/2 cup egg substitute
1/2 cup water
1/4 tsp. salt
2 Tbs. low-fat margarine

Place ingredients in blender in order named. Blend at high speed for 30 seconds. Scrape down sides. Blend another 60 seconds until smooth. (The batter can be mixed with an electric mixer.) Beat at high speed for three minutes. Let mixture cool in refrigerator for at least two hours. It will keep in the refrigerator for at least two days before using. Cook crepes according to directions of your crepe maker. If you don't have a crepe maker, do what I did and hint to your daughter that your birthday is coming up.

Chicken Curry Filling

3 cups diced cooked chicken breasts
I cup chicken broth, homemade, with fat extracted
I Tbs. low-fat margarine
2 Tbs. flour
2 tsp. curry powder
1/4 cup water chestnuts
I cup finely diced celery
I medium onion, chopped
1/2 tsp. salt
1/4 tsp. pepper
1/2 cup artificial sour cream

Melt margarine in a Teflon skillet. Sauté onions and celery. Add flour, salt, and pepper and mix well. Add chicken broth, and stir to get the lumps out. Add curry powder, diced chicken, water chestnuts, and pimiento. Mix well. I find it better to let the mixture cool in the refrigerator for a couple of hours, or it can be stored overnight. This way you can have a clean kitchen, and be rested up yourself before your guests arrive, because this is definitely company fare.

At least an hour before serving time, spoon two heaping Tbs. of chicken curry in the center of each cooked crepe with brown side under. Roll up like an enchilada and place in a baking dish. Bake in 350° oven for 20–25 minutes or until hot through. Serve with a dollop of artificial sour cream on top. Before my calorie-conscious-kick, I put toasted almonds on top. No more.

The crepes can be stuffed and rolled up the night before, and baked just before serving, or they can be baked ahead of time and heated in the microwave just before serving.

Try not to have more than 6 people at your dinner party, so that you can have some left over for the next day. Remember to serve these from the kitchen, or you won't have any left over anyway.

8 Servings of two crepes each: 245 Calories per Serving; 9 grams Fat; 96 mg. Cholesterol; 4 grams Saturated Fat.

Food Exchanges: 4 meat; 1 fat.

Curried Chicken

5 cups chicken broth (homemade)
4 tsp. curry powder
3 cups diced chicken (1 lb. of chicken breast)
3 carrots, sliced
2 celery ribs, chopped in 1/2-inch pieces
1/2 medium onion, chopped
1 apple, cored and chopped in 1/2-inch pieces
1/2 bell pepper, chopped
1/2 tsp. salt
1/4 tsp. pepper
3 cups hot cooked rice

Pour broth into a large skillet. Stir in curry powder and add chicken pieces. Add carrots, celery, onions, bell pepper, apple, salt, and pepper. Cook covered at medium heat. Stir occasionally, turning chicken over to cook evenly. Cook for 45 minutes. Serve over hot rice, allowing a little over 1/3 cup rice per serving.

8 Servings: 226 Calories per Serving; 3 grams Fat; 49 mg. Cholesterol; 1 gram Saturated Fat.

Food Exchanges: 2-1/4 meat; 1 bread; 1 vegetable.

Easy Curried Chicken

1 can (10-3/4 oz.) Weight Watchers cream of
    chicken soup
1 can (10-3/4 oz.) Weight Watchers cream of
    mushroom soup
1/4 cup skim milk
4 chicken breast halves, skinned
1 tsp. curry powder

1/4 cup water chestnuts, sliced
2 Tbs. pimiento
Salt and pepper to taste
3 cups cooked rice

Cut skinned chicken in smaller pieces. Boil until tender. Save stock for other uses. Take chicken off the bone and cut into bite-size pieces.

Combine and heat soups and milk in a large skillet. Add diced chicken and seasoning. Add water chestnuts and pimiento. Simmer until chicken is heated through. Serve over rice, allowing 1/2 cup of rice per serving.

6 Servings: 281 Calories per Serving: 4 grams Fat; 77 mg. Cholesterol; 1 gram Saturated Fat.

Food Exchanges: 3 meat; 1-1/2 fat.

Fried Chicken

4 chicken breasts (3 oz.), or 4 thighs (2 oz.)
1/4 tsp. salt
1/4 tsp. pepper
1 cup of skim milk

Skin the chicken and cut off every visible sign of fat. Marinade chicken pieces in milk for 20 to 30 minutes, then take out and pat dry with a paper towel. Salt and pepper. Spray Teflon skillet with vegetable cooking spray and heat over medium heat. Place chicken pieces in skillet. Put on lid and cook at low temperature for about 30 minutes. Turn pieces occasionally. When chicken appears tender, take off lid, turn up heat, and brown on both sides.

4 Servings:
Breasts: 166 Calories per Serving; 4 grams Fat; 75 mg. Cholesterol; 1 Saturated Fat.

Food Exchanges: 3 meat.

Thighs: 125 Calories; 6 grams Fat; 54 mg. Cholesterol; 1 gram Saturated Fat.

Food Exchanges: 2 meat.

Try

—— King Ranch Chicken Casserole ——

This dish is so tasty that you will never miss the calories that we have taken out of the original recipe. If you are serving this to folks who don't care about calories, you should count on its serving only six, because some will want second helpings.

> 4 chicken breasts
> 1 can Weight Watchers cream of mushroom soup
> 1-1/2 cups chicken broth, homemade
> 1 Tbs. flour
> 1 can Rotel tomatoes (stewed tomatoes with
>   peppers)
> 4 single slices of cheese (Weight Watchers)
> 8 corn tortillas
> 1 onion, chopped
> 1/2 tsp. salt
> 1 stalk celery

Skin the chicken breasts, remove all visible fat, place in large pot, and cover with water. Add a stalk of celery. Cook until tender. Take chicken out of water and debone. Put stock in refrigerator and cool. Skim fat from the top of the broth. Cut chicken into bite-size pieces.

Mix the flour with the chicken broth by putting one cup of the chicken broth and the flour in a jar with a lid and shake until blended. Add to remaining broth. Stir the mushroom soup until smooth, then mix with broth. Place half of the cut-up chicken pieces in a 9x12" casserole. Place one half of the tortillas, broken up in one-inch pieces, on top of the layer of chicken. Pour half of the broth and mushroom soup over the mixture; then add half of the Rotel tomatoes. Add half of the onions, then half of the cheese. Repeat the layers, ending with cheese on top. Bake in preheated oven at 350° for one hour.

Serves 8: 219 Calories per Serving; 6 grams Fat; 48 mg. Cholesterol; 2 grams Saturated Fat.

Food Exchanges: 2 meat; 1 bread; 1/2 fat; 1/2 vegetable.

Mexican Chicken Mole

I have not included many Mexican dishes in this book for several reasons: Most of our familiar Mexican dishes are more Tex-Mex than Mexican; most are difficult to take the calories out of and retain the flavor; and most are not the foods which the country Mexicans eat anyway. Chicken Mole is an exception. I hope you will like this truly Mexican dish, which, as far as I know, has not hit the Tex-Mex fast food circuit.

Mole can also be used for leftover turkey, or for wild geese and ducks.

    1 Tbs. vegetable oil
    1 bell pepper, seeded and chopped
    1 red pepper, seeded and chopped
    2 medium onions, chopped
    2 cloves garlic, crushed
    2 cans (15 oz.) tomato sauce
    4 tsp. chili powder
    1/4 tsp. cayenne
    1/2 tsp. salt
    4 whole cloves
    3 Tbs. cocoa powder
    3 Tbs. water
    2 cups cooked chicken breasts, diced

In a large skillet, sauté bell pepper, red pepper, onion, and garlic until slightly brown.

Dissolve cocoa in 3 Tbs. of water until smooth. Add dissolved cocoa, spices, and tomato sauce. Bring to a boil and simmer covered for another ten minutes, or until chicken is heated thoroughly.

6 Servings: 204 Calories per Serving; 7 grams Fat; 64 mg. Cholesterol; 2 grams Saturated Fat.

Food Exchanges: 2-1/2 meat; 2 vegetable.

—— Mexican Rice and Chicken ——

    4 chicken breasts (skinned and with all fat
        removed)
    6 cups water
    1 cup uncooked rice (regular, not instant)
    1 onion, chopped
    1 bell pepper, chopped
    2 garlic cloves

1/2 jalapeño (fresh or canned) or 4 chili pequins
1 Tbs. vegetable cooking oil
3 medium tomatoes, fresh, or 15 oz. canned
    tomatoes
4 carrots cut in one-inch chunks

Boil the skinned and defatted chicken breasts in 6 cups of water until tender. Put aside.

Heat the cooking oil in Teflon skillet. Brown the rice in the oil, stirring frequently to insure a uniform light brown. Put rice in another pan while you sauté the onion, bell pepper, and chopped garlic. Add the browned rice. Pour 4 cups of the chicken stock into the rice. Add cubed tomatoes, carrots, and jalapeños. Place chicken pieces on top. Put on a tight lid and cook for about 30 minutes. You may want to debone the chicken before adding to the rice.

6 Servings: 286 Calories per Serving; 5 grams Fat; 56 mg. Cholesterol; 2 grams Saturated Fat.

Food Exchanges: 2-1/2 meat; 1-3/4 bread; 2 vegetable.

Oven "Fried Chicken"

This method of frying chicken may be used for fish, pork chops, and chicken-fried steak.

> 4 chicken breasts
> 1/2 cup cornflake crumbs (made from 1 cup cornflakes*)
> 1 cup of skim milk
> Salt
> Pepper
> 1/2 tsp. Mrs. Dash
> 1/2 tsp. sweet basil

Skin the chicken and cut away all visible signs of fat. Marinate chicken breasts in milk for 15 or 20 minutes. Roll cornflakes into coarse crumbs. Take chicken out of marinade, salt and pepper, and add Mrs. Dash and sweet basil. Roll chicken in cornflake crumbs. Place pieces of chicken in shallow baking dish which has been coated with vegetable cooking spray. Place uncovered in 400° oven and cook for approximately 25 minutes. Check occasionally for tenderness.

*Charge yourself with only 1/2 cup of cornflakes because not all of it sticks on the meat, and with only 1/2 cup of milk.

> Serves 4: 170 Calories per Serving; 3 grams Fat; 73 mg. Cholesterol; 1 gram Saturated Fat.
>
> Food Exchanges: 3 meat.

Oven-Fried Cinnamon Chicken

2 chicken breast halves
2 chicken thighs
1/4 tsp. salt
1/2 tsp. pepper
2 Tbs. flour
1/4 tsp. tumeric
1 tsp. cinnamon
2 egg whites
1/2 cup cornflake crumbs (1 cup cornflakes)
1 tsp. vegetable oil

Mix salt, pepper, and flour in a small brown paper sack. In a small bowl, slightly beat the egg whites and add tumeric and cinnamon. Place one piece of chicken at a time in the brown paper sack and shake to coat with flour. Dip the chicken in the egg whites and then coat with the cornflakes.

Place chicken pieces in a heavy baking pan or Dutch oven and bake in a pre-heated 400° oven for about thirty minutes.

4 Servings: 183 Calories per Serving; 6 grams Fat; 61 mg. Cholesterol; 0 Saturated Fat.

Food Exchanges: 3 meat; 1/2 bread.

FISH

When we lived in a Maryland suburb of Washington, D.C., my special "dining out" entree was Crab Imperial. I savored it at several of the fine restaurants in the area, but my very favorite Crab Imperial was found at a modestly priced seafood restaurant near my office where we occasionally went for lunch. On my last day of work before moving back to Texas, my staff at the Department of Human Services took me to lunch at the seafood restaurant, where I ordered my favorite Crab Imperial for the last time.

Carried away in the excitement of the moment—regret in leaving my friends, coupled with anticipation of moving back to Texas—I asked to speak with the chef who had prepared this delicacy. I explained to him that I was moving to the Texas Coast and desperately wanted his recipe for Crab Imperial. The chef hummed and hawed, anxiously eyeing the ever-increasing lunch-hour line of people waiting to be seated. He didn't think it was possible to provide me with the recipe. It wasn't a pretty sight to see a grown woman beg.

Finally the young man leaned over and sheepishly whispered to me. "We put the crabmeat in a ramekin, spoon some Kraft's Miracle Whip over it, plunk it in the oven until the Miracle Whip bubbles, then serve it."

The chef grinned at me as he confessed further, "I'm not really a chef. I'm a student at Georgetown University. Right now, I'm working as a short-order cook."

I had imagined that hours and hours had gone into this secret recipe. It always seemed to me that the Chesapeake Bay crabs—and the Texas Coast crabs, for that matter — deserved better than that. So I always jazz it up a bit with pimientos and capers, or whatever.

If you live on the coast, or vacation on the coast, sidle up to an old-timer who can direct you to a favorite crab hole; get a crab net, a string, and some chicken necks from the grocery store. Net yourself a dozen crabs, being careful to keep them alive until you get home. Put on a big pot of water and drop the live crabs into it when it boils. Ask a local expert how to crack the crabs and pick out the meat.

Get yourself a jar of Miracle Whip Light. Voilá! Crab Imperial. A gourmet's delight.

Crabmeat is so expensive now that for awhile my supermarket did not carry it. They did carry the fake crabmeat, white fish seasoned to taste sorta like crabmeat. I tried it with my Crab Imperial recipe and it was not bad. My supermarket carries crabmeat now at $16 per pound. I sometimes act like a big-time spender and buy one fourth of a pound, which makes a nice quick dinner for me and my husband.

Sixteen dollars a pound makes me remember the time when my kids were the right age for family camping trips and we took them to North Carolina's Outer Banks for a week of camping at the beach. The second night there, we survived the most horrendous storm I had ever been in. The next morning my son wanted one last walk on the beach, because I had announced that we were getting out of there as soon as the ferry started to run. Down at the beach, the waves were bringing blue crab in to the shore by the bushels. I used my thongs for the crabs to cling to as we picked them up. In no time at all we had a bushel of big beautiful blue crabs. Enrapt in the sheer pleasure of having so many crabs, I forgot all about

how scared I had been the night before, when I had prayed
earnestly that God would save our children but he didn't have
to bother about saving their father and me, who did not deserve
to be saved—we had taken three children tenting on an island
on the Outer Banks, with no escape but by a daytime ferry.

We went down to the small village and bought a five-
gallon lard can, in which we boiled our crab catch.* My husband and I picked out crabmeat all day long. Our fingers were
bleeding from the ordeal. We got so sick of the crab that we
could not eat any of it. Instead, we greeted all new campers
that day with a pint of picked-out crabmeat. We must have
given away a couple of hundred dollars worth of fresh picked
crabmeat. Oh well, we didn't have any Miracle Whip anyway.

---

*I am not recommending a lard can as a suitable boiling pot.

Crab Imperial

8 oz. container of crabmeat, fresh or frozen
3 Tbs. Miracle Whip, Light (50% less calories)
1/4 cup low-fat yogurt
2 Tbs. pimiento
1 tsp. Worcestershire sauce
1 tsp. capers (optional)
4 slices of bread (40 calories per slice)

Check the crabmeat for possible pieces of shell. Add pimiento,
Worcestershire sauce, and fold in the Miracle Whip and yogurt.
Lightly toast 4 pieces of bread, and cut diagonally. Place two halves
of toast upright in individual ramekins. Spoon crab mixture into
ramekins. Place in 350° oven and bake until the Miracle Whip
begins to bubble—about 10 or 15 minutes.

4 Servings: 124 Calories per Serving; 4 grams Fat; 59 mg. Cholesterol; 0.8 grams Saturated Fat.

Food Exchanges: 1 meat; 1 fat; 1/2 bread.

Baked Crab Casserole

2 egg whites, slightly beaten
4 oz. cooked crabmeat
1/4 cup chopped bell pepper
3 Tbs. pimiento, chopped
1/2 tsp. mustard
1/4 tsp. Worcestershire sauce
1 Tbs. onion, chopped
2 Tbs. mayonnaise, Miracle Whip, Light
2 Tbs. egg substitute
1 slice reduced-calorie bread, made into crumbs
1/4 tsp. garlic powder

Combine egg whites and next six ingredients in a mixing bowl. Pour into a small baking dish. Combine egg substitute and mayonnaise and beat thoroughly. Spread over crab mixture. Top with bread crumbs. Sprinkle garlic on top and bake in 400° oven for 15 minutes.

2 Servings: 217 Calories per Serving; 13 grams Fat; 65 mg. Cholesterol; 2 grams Saturated Fat.

Food Exchanges: 2 meat; 2 fat.

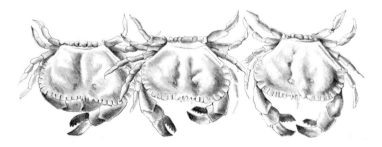

Try

Baked Fish

1 lb. of fish filet
1/2 cup skim milk
Pinch of salt
Pepper
1/2 tsp. sweet cumin
1/2 cup cornflakes, coarsely crushed
1/2 tsp. Mrs. Dash

Marinate fish in skim milk for ten minutes. Sprinkle salt, pepper, sweet cumin, and Mrs. Dash over the fish filets. Dredge fish in crushed cornflakes. Coat shallow baking dish with vegetable cooking spray. Place fish in baking dish, and bake in 450° oven for 12 to 15 minutes.

4 Servings: 136 Calories per Serving; 2 grams Fat; 42 mg. Cholesterol; 0.4 grams Saturated Fat.

Food Exchanges: 2-1/2 meat.

Try

Fish Foil Bake

1 lb. whitefish or orange roughy (4 filets)
2 Tbs. low-fat margarine
1/2 cup chopped parsley
2 Tbs. dill weed
2 Tbs. chopped chives
1/4 cup finely chopped onion
2 Tbs. lemon juice
1/4 tsp. salt
Pepper to taste

Rinse fish and pat dry with paper towel. Sprinkle lightly with salt.

Make stuffing by melting margarine in Teflon skillet. Add parsley, dill weed, chives, onion, and lemon juice. Place the stuffing on top side of filets. Roll up each filet and place in a separate piece of foil, carefully sealing the edges. Place in a baking dish, and bake in pre-heated 400° oven for 20 minutes. Unwrap and serve on a hot platter.

4 Servings: 164 Calories per Serving; 5 grams Fat; 94 mg. Cholesterol; 0.9 Saturated Fat.

Food Exchanges: 3 meat.

—— California Barbecued Salmon ——

My California daughter-in-law, Tule, served this to us when we visited there. This has to be the best fish I have ever tasted, which says a lot for someone who lived on the Texas Coast for many years. If you have a piece of the salmon left over (which I seriously doubt, unless you put some back) you can use this the next day to make hors d'oeuvres by spreading small bits of salmon on saltines with just a tiny bit of the dill sauce.

Fresh salmon does not come cheap, even on the West Coast, and certainly not in Central Texas where I live. But go ahead. Live dangerously. Sell the farm, if you must. You just have to try this recipe for barbecued salmon. Invite your best friends over for a cook-out and surprise them with barbecued fresh salmon.

> *2 lbs. fresh salmon filets (6 filets)*
> *2 tsp. dill weed*
> *1 tsp. garlic powder*

Sprinkle salmon filets with dill weed and garlic powder. Place in marinade for at least one hour.

Marinade

>Juice of one lemon
>2 cups white wine

While salmon is marinating, get coals ready in the barbecue grill. Have the cooking grill about five inches from the hot coals.

Take salmon out of marinade and pat dry. Place salmon skin-side down on the grill—or use a special fish holder. Grill salmon five minutes on one side. Turn, then grill about five minutes on other side. Lift carefully and place on hot platter. Serve immediately with dill sauce.

6 Servings: 290 Calories per Serving; 11 grams Fat; 75 mg. Cholesterol; 2 grams Saturated Fat.

Food Exchanges: 5 meat.

Dill Sauce

>1/2 cup Miracle Whip, Light
>1/4 cup Grey Poupon mustard
>1/2 tsp. dill weed

Mix ingredients together and beat with fork or small hand-beater.

Makes 12 Tablespoons: 18 Calories per Tablespoon; 2 grams Fat; 1 gram Cholesterol; 0.3 Saturated Fat.

Food Exchanges: 1/2 fat.

——— Salmon Croquettes ———

Given the price of salmon following the Alaskan oil spill, you would not be surprised that salmon was such a special treat when I was a child. Salmon was inexpensive then, about twenty-five cents a can, but that was twenty cents more than we had to spend. So, during cotton-picking season when we had a little cash, we had salmon croquettes every other Saturday night, alternating with fried bologna sausage the next Saturday night. Other times of the year, we had to make do on pork chops, steaks, sausage, and chicken.

Salmon croquettes is still a special treat for my husband.

> 1 can (15 oz.) salmon
> 1/4 cup chopped onions
> 2 slices of bread (40 calories per slice)
> 1/2 cup egg substitute
> 3/4 tsp. lemon pepper
> 1 cup coarsely crushed cornflakes
>   (2 cups of cornflakes)

Crush cornflakes by putting them in a plastic bag and then rolling lightly with a rolling pin. 2 cups makes about 1 cup of crushed crumbs.

Crumble the bread. Mix all ingredients except cornflakes together. Mixture will be soft and difficult to hold together. Make patties about 3 inches in diameter and 1 inch thick. Coat with crushed cornflakes. Place in baking dish coated with vegetable cooking spray and cook in 400° oven for 20 minutes, or place in nonstick skillet and pan fry.

NOTE: If your family does not need to restrict calories or cholesterol, roll their patties in your favorite cracker crumbs and fry in cooking oil.

5 Servings of two patties per serving: 170 Calories per Serving; 6 grams Fat; 36 mg. Cholesterol; 1 gram Saturated Fat.

Food Exchanges: 3 meat; 1 fat; 1 bread.

Jmy

—————————— Salmon Soufflé ——————————

2 tsp. low-cal margarine
2 Tbs. flour
1 cup skim milk
1/4 cup frozen egg substitute
1/4 tsp. salt
1/4 tsp. nutmeg
1/4 tsp. black pepper
1 (15-1/2 oz.) can of salmon
2 stiff-beaten egg whites

Make white sauce of margarine, flour, and milk. Slowly add sauce to thawed egg substitute. Add salt, nutmeg, pepper, and salmon. Fold in stiffly-beaten egg whites. Pour into casserole dish which has been coated with vegetable cooking spray. Bake in moderate oven (325°) for 45 minutes. Serve immediately.

6 Servings: 153 Calories per Serving; 6 grams Fat; 30 mg. Cholesterol; 1.5 grams Saturated Fat.

Food Exchanges: 3 meat.

—————————— Shrimp Jambalaya ——————————

2 lbs. shrimp, shelled and deveined
1/2 tsp. salt
1 bay leaf
2 Tbs. vegetable oil
1 medium bell pepper, seeded and chopped
6 scallions, with part of their green tops, chopped
4 stalks celery, chopped
1 Tbs. celery leaves, chopped
3 Tbs. flour
2 cups chicken stock, homemade, with fat
   skimmed from top

1/2 tsp. Tabasco sauce
1-1/2 cups lean cooked ham, diced
1 cup cooked chicken, diced
2 doz. oysters with their liquor
4 cups cooked rice
1/4 cup fresh parsley, minced

Place shelled and deveined shrimp in a pot of boiling water to which you have already added salt and bay leaf. Let come to a boil again and cook for about one minute. Leave shrimp in the pot to cool.

In a large Teflon skillet, heat vegetable oil. Sauté bell pepper, scallions, and celery. Add celery leaves. Blend in flour until it has browned slightly. Stir in chicken stock and cook for three minutes, stirring constantly until well blended. Add 1/2 cup of the liquid that shrimp was cooked in. Add Tabasco. Stir in ham and chicken. Cook for five minutes. Stir in oysters and their liquor. Cook until oysters are plump. Add drained shrimp and cooked rice. Blend well. Continue cooking until shrimp and rice are thoroughly heated. Serve on heated platter and sprinkle with parsley.

12 Servings: 242 Calories per Serving; 5 grams Fat; 177 mg. Cholesterol; 1 gram Saturated Fat.

Food Exchanges: 3 meat; 1 bread.

Try

Tuna Casserole

5 oz. medium noodles, uncooked
2 cans (6-1/2 oz.) water-packed tuna
2 Tbs. Miracle Whip, Light
1 cup celery, chopped
1/2 cup onion, chopped
1/4 green pepper, chopped
1/4 cup pimiento, chopped
1/4 cup water chestnuts or jicama, diced
1/4 tsp. salt
2 cans (10-3/4 oz.) Weight Watchers cream of
    celery soup
1/2 cup skim milk
1/2 cup Velveeta cheese, grated

Cook noodles according to instructions on package. Sauté onion, green pepper, and jicama (if used instead of water chestnuts). Combine noodles with tuna, mayonnaise, vegetables (and water chestnuts), and salt. Pour into a 2-quart casserole that has been sprayed with vegetable cooking spray. Combine soup, milk, and cheese, and heat slowly until cheese has melted. Pour over tuna mixture. Bake for 20 minutes in pre-heated 425° oven.

10 Servings: 155 Calories per Serving; 4 grams Fat; 32 mg. Cholesterol; 1.2 grams Saturated Fat.

Food Exchanges: 1/2 bread; 1/2 meat; 1 fat.

Try

Tuna Macaroni

This makes a very good one-dish meal. Add a green salad and a fruit, and you have a satisfying meal for less than 300 calories.

> 2/3 cup uncooked macaroni
> 2 Tbs. Miracle Whip, Light
> 1 small onion, minced
> 1 Tbs. flour
> 1 cup skim milk
> 1 chicken bouillon cube
> 1/2 tsp. pepper
> 1 can (6-1/2 oz.) water-packed tuna
> 3 Tbs. pimientos
> 2 tsp. parsley flakes for garnish (optional)

In a two-quart saucepan, cook macaroni as directed on package. Drain and return macaroni to original saucepan. Keep warm.

Meanwhile, in a saucepan over medium heat, melt margarine; add onion, and sauté until tender, stirring occasionally. Stir in flour until blended. Gradually stir in milk, bouillon, salt, and pepper. Cook until thickened and smooth, stirring constantly. Stir in tuna and pimientos; heat through. Gently toss macaroni in saucepan with tuna mixture. Leave on the stove until mixture is heated throughout. Spoon mixture into warmed bowl. Garnish with parsley.

6 Servings: 159 Calories per Serving; 3 grams Fat; 13 mg. Cholesterol; 0.6 grams Saturated Fat.

Food Exchanges: 1 meat; 1 bread; 1/2 fat.

BEEF ~~Iny~~

Chicken-Fried Steak and Cream Gravy

At first, I thought that I would not include Chicken-Fried Steak, because it is such a common food which everyone knows how to prepare, and is terribly fattening with all that grease. Then I remembered that Chicken-Fried Steak is not all that common in some parts of the country. Furthermore, the name of this book promises that I would take the calories out of country cooking. And so we have. You will find that you can fry lots of things in one teaspoon of oil.

I separated the calorie count of the steak from the gravy, because I know that some of you good folks up north don't like cream gravy. When I was promoting *Mrs. Blackwell's* in the Downtown Mall in Hartford, Connecticut, I cooked chicken-fried steak and gravy—the fattening way. I poured the gravy into a deep bowl with a small top. My "customers" took a bite-size piece of steak on a toothpick, and I asked them to dip it in the "sauce." They loved it. I have never told them until now that they were eating cream gravy.

>   2 steaks (4 oz. each), round, tenderized
>   2 Tbs. flour
>   1/4 cup skim milk
>   2 Tbs. egg substitute
>   1 tsp. vegetable oil
>   Salt
>   Pepper

Mix milk and egg substitute together in a shallow bowl. Add tenderized meat and let it marinate for about 30 minutes. Place flour, salt, and pepper in a plastic or paper bag. Take meat out of egg mixture and wipe off slightly. Place the meat in the paper bag, close top, and shake to coat with the flour.

Heat oil in Teflon skillet. Place steak in skillet; brown on one side, then turn. Continue cooking until meat is done to your satisfaction.

Take meat up and keep warm while you prepare the gravy.

2 Servings: 141 Calories per Serving; 9 grams Fat; 36 mg. Cholesterol; 0 Saturated Fat.

Food Exchanges: 2 meat; 1/2 fat.

Gravy

    1 Tbs. wheat flour
    1 cup skim milk
    Salt
    Pepper

Place milk and flour in a jar with a lid and shake until flour is blended. Pour into the skillet in which meat was cooked. Stir in all the meat crumbs left by the steak. Cook until gravy is thickened.

2 Servings: 57 Calories per Serving; 0.2 Fat; 2 mg. Cholesterol; 0.2 Saturated Fat.

Food Exchanges: 1/2 milk.

Fry

Beef Patty Meal-in-One

1 lb. ground round beef
1/4 tsp. Mrs. Dash
1/8 tsp. pepper
4 carrots
1/2 cup celery, chopped
1/2 medium onion, chopped
1 clove garlic
1/2 cup bell pepper, sliced
1 medium zucchini, in one-inch slices
1/2 cup fresh or canned mushrooms
1 Tbs. Kikkoman Lite Soy Sauce, or Worcestershire sauce
1 pkt. sugar substitute

Make four patties. Brown meat on both sides in large Teflon frying pan sprayed with vegetable cooking spray. Take patties out of pan and set aside. Sauté mushrooms, onions, pepper, celery, and garlic. Add meat, cut-up carrots, and zucchini. Sprinkle soy sauce and one pkt. of sugar substitute over meat and vegetables. Add 1/2 cup water, and cook until meat and vegetables are done to taste.

4 Servings: 239 Calories per Serving; 6 grams Fat; 71 mg. Cholesterol; 2 grams Saturated Fat.

Food Exchanges: 4 meat; 1 vegetable.

Beef Stroganoff

1 lb. beef tenderloin
1/4 tsp. salt
Pepper
1 cup mushrooms, sliced
1 onion, chopped
2 Tbs. vegetable oil
3 Tbs. flour
2 cups beef bouillon
2 Tbs. tomato paste
1 tsp. dry mustard
1/4 tsp. oregano
1/4 tsp. dill weed
1/3 cup low-fat yogurt

Remove all visible fat from meat and cut in thin strips about 2 inches long. In a Teflon skillet, sauté mushrooms in oil until tender. Remove from skillet and sauté onions until clear. Remove. Brown meat quickly on all sides. Remove and set aside. Blend flour into oil in skillet, and gradually add bouillon, stirring constantly until smooth and slightly thick. Add tomato paste, dry mustard, oregano, and dill weed. Blend well. Return steak, mushrooms, and onion to skillet with sauce, and cook for 20 minutes. Blend in yogurt 5 minutes before serving.

4 Servings: 320 Calories per Serving: 17 grams Fat; 84 mg. Cholesterol; 4 grams Saturated Fat.

Food Exchanges: 4 meat; 1 vegetable; 1-1/2 fat.

Cabbage Patch Stew

1 lb. ground lean meat
1 tsp. vegetable oil
1 bell pepper
2 stalks celery, cut in 1" pieces
1 large onion
2 garlic buds
1 can (15 oz.) ranch-style beans
1 can (15 oz.) tomatoes
1 can (15 oz.) whole corn
1 Tbs. Worcestershire sauce
2 Tbs. chili powder
1 head cabbage
Salt to taste

Cut cabbage in 3-inch chunks and put in cold water to crisp.

Brown ground meat in Teflon skillet in the vegetable oil. When brown, take meat out, and sauté bell pepper, onion, garlic buds, and celery.

Transfer meat and sautéed vegetables to a large pot. Add one can of ranch-style beans, 1 can tomatoes, and 1 can of whole corn. Add Worcestershire sauce and chili powder. Bring to a boil and let simmer for a couple of hours. About forty minutes before serving, take cabbage out of water, dry with a towel, and place in the pot. Continue cooking for 40 or 45 minutes.

This is a one-dish meal, but can serve about 20 people at the local Presbyterian Church potluck luncheons.

10 Servings: 206 Calories per Serving; 4 grams Fat; 30 mg Cholesterol; 3.4 grams Saturated Fat.

Food Exchanges: 2 meat; 1/2 bread; 1 vegetable; 1 fat.

Chili con Carne #1

1-1/2 lbs. diced beef (all fat removed)
2 tsp. olive oil
2 medium onions, chopped
1/2 cup bell peppers, chopped
1 (10 oz.) can of tomatoes, with liquid
1-1/2 Tbs. chili powder
1/4 tsp. ground cumin
2 cloves of garlic, minced
1/4 tsp. salt
Black pepper to taste
1/8 tsp. oregano
2-4 drops of Tabasco sauce, or Louisiana hot
    sauce
1 cup canned kidney beans, drained

Heat olive oil in large skillet. Brown diced beef. Put beef and all other ingredients except kidney beans in a Crockpot. Cook on low for 6 to 8 hours. While the chili is cooking, you can go swimming, shopping, and whatever else you need to do. Just get home in time to add the beans for the last hour. You can let this cook overnight if you care to.

This, of course, can be cooked on top of the stove in a heavy pot. Have temperature on medium until mixture begins to bubble. Set on very low heat and cook for several hours. Be sure to check frequently and to stir. If cooked on top of stove, mixture will need water added, so you can't leave it to go shopping.

8 Servings: 295 Calories per Serving; 17 grams Fat; 74 mg. Cholesterol; 6 grams Saturated Fat.

Food Exchanges: 3 meat; 1/2 bread; 1 vegetable; 1 fat.

Chili con Carne #2

1-1/2 cups cooked red chili beans, or kidney beans
1 large onion, chopped
1 bell pepper, chopped
1 lb. ground lean beef
3-1/2 cups of canned tomatoes
1/2 tsp. salt
1/8 tsp. paprika
1/8 tsp. cayenne pepper
3 whole cloves
1 bay leaf
1-1/2 Tbs. chili powder

Brown onions, bell pepper, and meat in skillet. Transfer to a pot. Add tomatoes and seasoning. Simmer 2 or 3 hours, adding water if necessary. Add beans the last hour of cooking.

You may use a Crockpot, but allow more time for cooking.

8 Servings: 250 Calories per Serving; 10 grams Fat; 109 mg. Cholesterol; 3.7 grams Saturated Fat.

Food Exchanges: 2 meat; 1 bread; 1 vegetable.

Salisbury Steak

1-1/2 cups skim milk
1 Tbs. low-fat margarine
1 Tbs. plus 1 tsp. flour
1 Tbs. prepared mustard
2 tsp. Worcestershire sauce
1 tsp. prepared horseradish (optional)
1/4 cup mushrooms, fresh or canned
1-1/2 pounds lean ground beef

1/8 cup frozen egg substitute, thawed
1/4 cup dry bread crumbs (4 slices of bread, 40
   calories each)
1/4 cup onion, finely chopped
1/4 tsp. salt
1/4 tsp. pepper
1/2 cup water
2 Tbs. parsley, chopped

Cream flour in 1 tablespoon of margarine. Add milk to make a cream sauce. Add mustard, Worcestershire sauce, horseradish, and mushrooms. Blend well. In a bowl, combine ground meat, frozen egg substitute, bread crumbs, onion, salt, pepper, and 1/4 cup of the cream sauce. Shape into six patties and brown in a separate Teflon skillet coated with vegetable cooking spray. Combine cream sauce, water, and parsley, and pour over patties. Cook over medium to low heat for 20 minutes, stirring the gravy occasionally.

8 Servings: 268 Calories per Serving; 15 grams Fat; 72 mg. Cholesterol; 8 grams Saturated Fat.

Food Exchanges: 3 meat; 2 fat.

Ground turkey may be substituted for the beef. Calories would be reduced to: 191 Calories per Serving; 10.5 Fat; 74.5 mg. Cholesterol; 6 grams Saturated Fat.

Food Exchanges: 3 meat; 1 fat.

Doesn't taste like mix but is good.

———————— Sloppy Joes ————————

1 lb. ground beef (round)
1/2 cup onions, chopped
1/2 cup celery, chopped
1 cup (8 oz.) tomato sauce
1 clove garlic, minced
1/4 tsp. salt
1/8 tsp. pepper
1/8 tsp. red pepper
6 medium hamburger buns

Could do this part then add Commercial sloppy joe spice packet for heat.

Sauté ground beef, onion, celery, and garlic. Drain any excess fat by use of a paper towel. Add tomato sauce, salt, and pepper. Simmer at least ten minutes. You may substitute ground turkey for the ground beef.

In the meantime, heat hamburger buns in oven or toaster oven. Spoon hamburger mixture over both pieces of each bun. You can cut down on the calories by using only one bun.

6 Servings:

Whole bun and beef: 326 Calories per Serving; 15 grams Fat; 63 mg. Cholesterol; 5 grams Saturated Fat.

Food Exchanges: 3 meat; 2 bread; 1 fat.

One-half bun and beef: 269 Calories; 15 grams Fat; 63 mg. Cholesterol; 5 grams Saturated Fat.

Food Exchanges: 3 meat; 1 bread; 1 fat.

Ground turkey and whole bun: 296 Calories; 12 grams Fat; 63 mg. Cholesterol; 0.3 grams Saturated Fat.

Food Exchanges: 3 meat; 2 bread.

Smothered Steak

1 lb. round steak
Salt and pepper
2 Tbs. flour
1 Tbs. vegetable oil
2 cups hot water
1/2 cup onion, chopped

Trim all visible fat from steak. Cut into four serving pieces. Pound on both sides to tenderize. (If you don't have a tenderizing hammer, use the back side of the blade of a large butcher knife.) Salt and pepper. Put flour in a medium-size paper bag and add pieces of steak; close the open end, and shake. Flour will be evenly distributed on the meat.

Heat oil in a skillet. Place floured steak in oil and brown on both sides. Add onions and sauté them along with the meat. Add 1-1/2 cups of hot water. Cover tightly with lid and simmer until meat is tender. Add additional water if necessary.

4 Servings: 181 Calories per Serving; 8 grams Fat; 57 mg. Cholesterol; 2 grams Saturated Fat.

Food Exchanges: 3 meat; 1/2 milk.

Sukiyaki

1 lb. tenderloin steak
1 Tbs. vegetable oil
1 beef bouillon cube in 1/4 cup water
1-1/2 tsp. honey
1/4 cup lite soy sauce
1/2 cup green onions, cut diagonally in 1/2-inch
  lengths
1/2 cup celery, cut diagonally into 1-inch lengths
1/2 cup mushrooms, thinly sliced
2 cups fresh spinach leaves
1 cup water chestnuts, drained and sliced
1 cup bamboo shoots, drained and slivered
1 cup bean sprouts, drained and rinsed in water

For best results, use partially-frozen steak for slicing. Remove excess fat. Using sharp knife, slice meat in very thin slices across grain diagonally from top to bottom. Before cooking, have all vegetables prepared. Preheat large electric nonstick fry pan to 400°. Heat oil in pan. Quickly sauté steak strips a few at a time until browned on both sides (about 2 minutes). Combine beef bouillon, soy sauce, and honey, and pour over cooked steak strips. Push the meat to one side of the pan. Allow the sauce to begin bubbling. Add the onions, celery, and mushrooms. Cook on high heat for 2 minutes. Push aside each as it is cooked. Add the remaining vegetables in the same manner. Season with pepper. Add 1/4 cup water if needed. Serve immediately with rice, allowing 1/2 cup rice per serving.

8 Servings: 274 Calories per Serving; 7 grams Fat; 48 mg. Cholesterol; 0 Saturated Fat.

Food Exchanges: 2 meat; 1-1/2 bread; 1 vegetable; 1/2 fat.

Swiss Steak

Back on the farm this was a good way to cook steak from range cattle which had not been fattened up for the kill. Since we are going to cut away all visible signs of fat, it is still a good way to cook the less tender cuts of steak.

2 lbs. round steak, one-inch thick
1/4 cup flour
1/2 tsp. salt
1/2 tsp. pepper
1 Tbs. vegetable oil
1 medium onion, sliced
1/2 medium bell pepper, chopped
1 clove of garlic
1 cup canned tomatoes
1/4 cup mushrooms, optional

Cut away all visible signs of fat. Tenderize steak by pounding with a meat mallet. Dredge it in a mixture of the flour, salt, and pepper. Heat vegetable oil in nonstick skillet. Brown meat on both sides in vegetable oil. Add onion, garlic, and green pepper and cook until onions are clear. Add tomatoes and 1 cup of boiling water. Simmer, covered, for about one hour. Place steak on serving plate. Spoon sauce over top.

8 Servings: 160 Calories per Serving; 1 gram Fat; 53 mg. Cholesterol; 2 grams Saturated Fat.

Food Exchanges: 3 meat; 1 vegetable.

TURKEY

In *Mrs. Blackwell's Heart of Texas Cookbook*, I tell how my mother boiled the holiday turkey and made cornbread dressing on the side. My publisher, David Bowen, who immigrated from New York to Texas, was aghast.

"Boil the turkey?" he asked incredulously.

I explained that the turkeys who roamed the fields and pastures foraging for food were tough ol' birds—too tough to stuff and roast. They had to be boiled slowly for a very long time to make them tender enough to chew. Although I am not now recommending that you boil the holiday bird, you could take out lots of calories if you skinned the turkey, then boiled it. You could let the fat rise to the top of the broth, and skim it off before using the broth to make the dressing and giblet gravy. However, that idea wouldn't fly with my family at Thanksgiving. They enjoy the presentation of the golden brown turkey, the crown jewel of the holiday season, and the attendant turkey carving ritual.

In my first recipe book, I wrote that you must first catch the turkey. Then you kill, pluck, and dress it, and over an open fire you singe the hair and pinfeathers.

Scratch that monkey business! I was recreating the way it was during my childhood, back during the Depression era. We're in the last decade of the twentieth century. Times have changed, and turkeys have changed. Your turkey now comes killed, plucked, dressed, trussed, basted, and often with a little thingamajig that pops up when it is done. Believe me when I say, "Enjoy." You don't even want to know about chopping the turkey's head off, to say nothing of those pesky, pervasive pinfeathers.

When you select your holiday bird, or when you're given one by the corporate boss, read and follow the instructions about thawing time and cooking time. Always allow a little more cooking time than you expect to need. Frequent opening of the oven by family and friends to check on the holiday bird tends to slow down the cooking process.

I have always prepared the stuffing the night before, but have waited until morning to spoon it into the turkey.

Most recipes call for rubbing cavities with salt. Use salt sparingly or use Mrs. Dash instead.

Spoon the stuffing or dressing into the large cavity and the neck cavity. Close the openings by use of skewers and lacing—or by sewing, as I do. I usually use a large carpet needle with strong thread and sew the skin in place so that the stuffing will not tumble out. Sometimes I use drapery pins, which work very well by bending them to whatever position needed to secure the stuffing.

This year I will extricate a bunch of the calories from the stuffing, place part of the stuffing in the bird as usual, and cook the remainder on the side for those of us who do not need the extra calories which the juices from the turkey add.

After you have stuffed the bird, tuck the wings behind the shoulder joints. Tuck the drumsticks in the hole just above the tail. Place foil tightly over the legs and wings. This will prevent them from becoming too brown and hard before the rest of the bird is done. Place the turkey breast-up on a rack in a large roasting pan. Place a sheet of foil loosely over the top. If you use a baking thermometer, stick it in a thick part of the breast. Bake in a 300° oven, allowing about 30 minutes per pound for a smaller bird and about 20 to 25 minutes for larger birds. The meat thermometer should register around

190°. A way to test doneness is to take the drumstick and move it up and down; if the leg part seems to pull away from the torso, the turkey is done. If there is a little thingamajig that pops up, fine, but don't depend upon it entirely. A more accurate barometer is when your family declares that they are starving and are even willing to turn off the televised football game if you'll only hurry up dinner.

For the past two years I have bought turkey breasts. Most people prefer white meat, even those not watching calories. The turkey breast can be stuffed and roasted just like a whole turkey, and makes an attractive presentation.

I have given you a great recipe for giblet gravy, without all that grease. I have also given you two choices of holiday stuffing—bread stuffing and cornbread dressing. There are many more kinds, almost as many as there are cooks. It is the cornbread dressing vs. bread stuffing which divides the country; that is a dividing line more definitive than the Mason-Dixon Line. Ask a person what kind of stuffing he likes and you'll know whether he is from the north or south, long after the accents have been diffused. Some Southerners, however, may not know what you mean by "stuffing", and Yankees will not know what I mean by "dressing." Stuffing, dressing—cornbread or bread—let's take out as many calories as possible this holiday season!

While we are talking turkey, we are aware that our national holiday bird is not just for holidays anymore. The holiday bird of yore has been smoked, cured, wienered, chopped up, ground up, fileted, and fajitaed—all in the name of making us a fat-free society. When we talk turkey, we are talking about lowering cholesterol and excess poundage.

We have a few turkey recipes which you will want to try. You may also want to substitute ground turkey in most any recipe that calls for ground beef, including hamburgers, meatballs, meat loaf, and chili. You can also buy turkey sausage and bacon.

——— Caloric Value of Roast Turkey ———

4 oz. roasted breast, no skin: 153 Calories; 1 gram Fat; 95 mg. Cholesterol; 0.3 grams Saturated Fat.

Food Exchanges: 3-1/2 meat.

4 oz. roasted dark meat, no skin: 212 Calories; 8 grams Fat; 96 mg. Cholesterol; 3 grams Saturated Fat.

Food Exchanges: 4 meat.

You can have turkey (white meat), cornbread dressing, and giblet gravy for 305 calories; or turkey (dark meat), Holiday Bread Dressing, and gravy for 321 calories. No second helpings, please.

Gravy

You should boil the giblets the night before and put the stock in the refrigerator, where the fat rises to the top. Skim the fat off the top. You will be using 2 cups of broth. Take one cup, put it in a jar, and add 2 tablespoons flour. Put a lid on the jar and shake until flour is well blended. Add to the other cup of broth in a saucepan. Cook for five or ten minutes until gravy is thickened. Add salt and pepper to taste. If the gravy looks too anemic, add a beef bouillon cube to give it a headier taste and color. Makes 2 cups of gravy.

8 Servings: 17 Calories per Serving; 0.4 grams Fat; 2 mg. Cholesterol; 0.1 grams Saturated Fat.

Food Exchanges: 1 meat; 1 bread.

Giblet Gravy

If you add one cup of cut-up giblets to the two cups of gravy, you will have the following:

10 Servings: 38 Calories per Serving; 0.5 grams Fat; 61 mg. Cholesterol; 0.4 Saturated Fat.

Food Exchanges: 1 meat; 1 bread.

Holiday Bread Stuffing

1/2 cup chopped celery
1/2 cup chopped onions
2 Tbs. reduced-calorie margarine
6 cups dry bread cubes (40 calories per slice)
1 Tbs. chopped parsley, fresh or dried
1 bay leaf
1/2 tsp. salt
1/2 tsp. pepper
1 tsp. poultry seasoning
1/2 cup frozen egg substitute
3/4 cup skim milk
1 cup chicken broth (homemade, with fat
    skimmed off)

Cook celery and onion in margarine until soft, but not brown. Add bread cubes and parsley. Mix thoroughly. Add bay leaf, seasoning, and egg substitute. Heat the milk and broth separately. Add the liquid in sufficient amount to moisten the stuffing. This is enough stuffing for a 10- to 12-pound turkey.

You may add oysters if you like. Some of my family wanted oyster stuffing and others did not. I made up the basic recipe and put half of the stuffing in the lower cavity, then added oysters to the remaining stuffing and put that in the breast cavity. If you add oysters, be sure to count the additional calories, which are roughly 160 calories for a cupful, divided by 10, equals sixteen extra calories. Aw forget it, it's Christmas! You can have the oysters for free, if you can afford their cholesterol.

10 Servings: 81 Calories per Serving; 3-1/2 grams Fat; 0.7 mg. Cholesterol (without the oysters); 0.5 grams Saturated Fat.

Food Exchanges: 1 bread (without the oysters).

Cornbread Dressing

This is essentially the same recipe for cornbread dressing that my mother used to make, as recorded in *Mrs. Blackwell's Heart of Texas Cookbook*, except, of course, we have skimmed all fat from the turkey or chicken broth and have altered the recipe for the cornbread.

5 cups chicken broth, all fat skimmed from top
1 pan cornbread (see recipe below)
8 biscuits
2 eggs, hard boiled
1 medium onion, chopped
2/3 cup celery, chopped
1/2 tsp. salt
1 tsp. sage
1/2 tsp. black pepper

Cook onion and celery in broth for five minutes. Crumble cornbread and biscuit. Add salt, pepper, and sage to crumbled bread. Add onion, celery, and broth and stir until all bread is moist and soft. Add chopped boiled eggs. Beat by hand for one or two minutes. Dressing will be rather soft. Pepper and sage can be increased according to taste.

Pour into a two-quart baking dish and bake in 400° oven for about 45 minutes. Do not overbake. This dressing is probably too soft to stuff into the holiday bird before roasting. Where I grew up, most people baked the dressing separate from the hen or turkey. I presume that is why they do not call it 'stuffing', as people do up North.

12 Servings: 114 Calories per Serving; 5 grams Fat; 46 mg. Cholesterol; 1.3 grams Saturated Fat.

Food Exchanges: 1 bread; 1/2 fat.

Cornbread for Dressing

This cornbread is different from "Country Cornbread" on page 158, which is made with buttermilk and baking soda and is quite good. My mother never liked to use "soda cornbread", which is what she would have called "Country Cornbread", for dressing. Why, I cannot tell you, but we will go with her judgment. The recipe below is cornbread to be used in dressing, but I cannot recommend it for much of anything else.

> 1 cup cornmeal
> 1 cup flour
> 1/4 cup egg substitute
> 3 tsp. baking powder
> 1/2 tsp. salt
> 3 Tbs. vegetable oil
> 1-1/4 cups skim milk

Mix flour, meal, baking powder, and salt. Add milk, egg substitute, and vegetable oil. Pour into a 9x9" pan sprayed with vegetable cooking spray. Bake in 400° pre-heated oven for about 20 minutes.

Calories and food exchanges calculated with Cornbread Dressing.

Spaghetti and Meatballs

My daughter-in-law, Patti, who has just enough Italian blood to make her a darn good cook, gave me this recipe. She uses a different meat combination, more cheese and oil. She can afford it because she is a gorgeous size 6 with Irish red hair and Welsh complexion.

Meatballs

1/2 lb. lean ground beef
1/2 lb. ground turkey (456 calories)
1/4 cup onion, chopped
1/4 cup frozen egg substitute
3 bread slices (40 calories per slice)
1/4 cup skim milk
1 tsp. dried parsley or three stems of fresh parsley
1/2 tsp. oregano
1/2 tsp. garlic powder
1/2 tsp. coarsely ground pepper
1/2 tsp. salt

Mix all ingredients together and form 10 meatballs. Place on pan sprayed with vegetable cooking spray and brown in 400° oven for twenty minutes. Set aside.

Spaghetti Sauce

2 cans peeled and diced tomatoes (14-1/2 oz.)
1 can tomato paste (6 oz.)
1 can tomato sauce (8 oz.)
2 Tbs. sugar
1/2 tsp. Sweet'n Low
3 cloves garlic, cut up
1 tsp. oregano
1 tsp. sweet basil
3 sprigs of fresh parsley, or 1 tsp. ground
1/2 tsp. garlic powder
1/2 tsp. salt
2 oz. mozzarella cheese (160 calories)

Sauté garlic in olive oil in pan sprayed with vegetable cooking spray. Mix all ingredients in large pot. Add the meatballs and simmer for two hours.

Cook spaghetti according to directions on the package. Allow 3/4 cup per serving. Add spaghetti to calorie count.

10 Servings: 283 Calories per Serving; 5 grams Fat; 43 mg. Cholesterol; 2 grams Saturated Fat.

Food Exchanges: 2 meat; 2 bread; 1 vegetable.

Spaghetti: *114 Calories; 3/4 gram Fat; 0 Cholesterol; 0 Saturated Fat.*

Food Exchanges: 1 bread.

———— Stuffed Bell Pepper ————

3 medium bell peppers
8 oz. ground turkey
3/4 cup cooked rice
1/4 cup grated cheddar cheese (reduced fat)
1/2 cup onion, finely chopped
Salt
Pepper
1/2 tsp. sweet basil
1/2 tsp. Italian herbs
1 (4 oz.) can tomato sauce
1/4 cup egg substitute

Cut peppers in half lengthwise, and remove seeds. Simmer in salt water for 5 minutes. Combine cooked rice with remaining ingredients and stuff the peppers. Place upright in baking dish sprayed with vegetable cooking spray. Add a small amount of water for steaming. Cover and bake for 50 minutes at 350°. Serve with tomato sauce.

Tomato Sauce

1 No. 2 can (15 oz.) tomatoes
1 Tbs. chopped onion
1 Tbs. flour
2 tsp. dry Butter Buds
Salt and pepper to taste

Simmer tomatoes, onion, salt, and pepper together 10 minutes. Mix flour with 3 Tbs. water to make a paste. Gradually add the flour paste to tomato mixture. Add Butter Buds. Cook for about five more minutes, stirring constantly. Pour over peppers.

Bell peppers without sauce: 6 Servings: 127 Calories per Serving; 2 grams Fat; 34 mg. Cholesterol.

Food Exchanges: 1-1/2 meat; 1/2 bread; 1 vegetable.

Sauce: 6 Servings: 24 Calories per Serving; 0 Fat; 0 Cholesterol; 0 Saturated Fat.

Food Exchanges: 1 vegetable.

Turkey "Hamburgers"

8 oz. ground turkey (90% less fat)
4 hamburger buns
4 onion slices
8 pickle slices (sour or dill)
4 tomato slices
4 lettuce leaves
4 tsp. mustard
2 tsp. horseradish
1 tsp. Mrs. Dash
Pepper and salt to taste

Make four turkey patties. Sprinkle Mrs. Dash and pepper on the patties. Cook patties in Teflon skillet sprayed with vegetable cooking spray. In the meantime, open the buns and scoop out the equivalent of 1/2 of the bun from the two sides, being careful to leave the crusty outside intact. Place the buns in toaster oven to warm. When patties are done, plop them into the buns and add the other ingredients. Lots of Southern people prefer mayonnaise in their hamburger. Okay, if that turns you on, but you will have to add the mayonnaise calories to the total count.

If you want extra special hamburgers, simply substitute English muffins for the regular hamburger buns. Be sure to slice each side of the English muffin into two pieces and use outside pieces for the hamburgers. Save the inside pieces for morning toast.

4 Servings: 198 Calories per hamburger; 8 grams Fat; 48 mg. Cholesterol; 0.7 grams Saturated Fat.

Food Exchanges: 2 meat; 1 bread; 1 vegetable.

—— Turkey "Meat Loaf" Supreme ——

1 lb. ground turkey (90% less fat)
1/2 cup bell pepper, chopped
1/2 cup onion, chopped
1/2 cup mushrooms, chopped (fresh or canned)
2 slices bread (40 calories per slice)
1/4 cup water chestnuts
1/2 cup egg substitute
1 8-oz. can of tomato sauce
2 Tbs. Weight Watchers ketchup
2 garlic buds
1 tsp. sweet basil
1 tsp. lemon pepper
2 Tbs. Worcestershire sauce
1/2 tsp. salt

Crumble bread into cubes. Add all other ingredients except meat. Mix together. Then add meat. I don't know about you, but the only satisfactory way I've found to mix meat loaf is with my hands. This mixture will be soft and squooshy—too soft to mold into a mound like some people make meat loaf. Put the mixture into a 4x8″ loaf pan which has been sprayed with a vegetable spray. (I bought a new meat loaf pan which is perforated on the bottom and sits in a second pan just a tad bigger. This is designed to let the fat drip out into the second pan. Since this recipe doesn't have any fat to speak of, the special pan is not necessary but it is a nice contraption to have.) Bake in 350° oven for about 50 minutes.

You may delete the water chestnuts and/or the mushrooms—then you will have to delete the word, "Supreme." This will not make an appreciable difference in calories, just in price.

8 Servings: 163 Calories per Serving; 8 grams Fat; 48 mg. Cholesterol; 0.7 grams Saturated Fat.

Food Exchanges: 2 meat; 1 vegetable; 1 fat.

Turkey Pie

2 Tbs. low-fat margarine
1/4 tsp. salt
1/2 tsp. poultry seasoning
1/4 cup flour
1 cup turkey broth (fat removed)
1 cup skim milk
2 cups diced turkey
1 pkg. frozen mixed vegetables (carrots, peas, etc.)
1/2 cup chopped onion
Can of six biscuits

Melt margarine in saucepan. Blend in salt, poultry seasoning, and flour. Add turkey broth and milk. Bring to a boil, stirring constantly. Add turkey, frozen vegetables, and onion. Bring to boil again. Turn into a deep 2-qt. casserole and put six canned biscuits on top. Bake at 450° for 12–15 minutes, or until biscuits are brown.

6 Servings: 251 Calories per Serving; 9 grams Fat; 31 mg. Cholesterol; 3 grams Saturated Fat.

Food Exchanges: 1-2/3 meat; 1 bread; 1 vegetable; 1 fat.

Vegetables

VEGETABLES

In the chapter on meats and poultry, I suggested that most of you should not try to raise your own meat, poultry, and fish. (Although the father of my daughter-in-law Tule raises his own fish in his otherwise unused backyard swimming pool in Fresno, California, I personally think he might do better to swim in his pool and buy his fish at the market.) It is a different story with vegetables, if you have the space and inclination. Join the throngs of people who sit around at cocktail parties and brag about their tomatoes and squash. I am not a vegetable gardener, but some of my best friends are. My gardening consists of raising "food for the soul" as in tulips, begonias, pansies, petunias, and zinnias. But I'm a real sucker for the Farmers' Market anywhere, anytime. I have been known to backtrack as much as five or ten miles on the highway if I have inadvertently passed up a roadside stand.

Raise your own, beg vegetables from your gardening friends, buy them at roadside stands, or from the supermarket —just keep yourself supplied with plenty of fresh vegetables. Left to themselves, most vegetables are very low in calories and high in nutrients. No need to tell you how to take the calories *out* of vegetables. I am just going to try to encourage you not to put too many calories *in*.

There are two basic ways to cook vegetables—the "up North" version and the "down South" country version. My friends and my daughter-in-law up North steep the vegetables in hot water just long enough to heat through. My family down South cook vegetables slowly and for a very long time until they are soft and mushy. Take your pick. I won't take sides about how long to boil or steam vegetables. However, I will admit reluctantly that the "up North" way is healthier.

My mother always put a teaspoon of sugar in almost all vegetables as they cooked. We will add a sugar substitute, but only the kind that can be used in cooking. Unless you are on a rigid sugar-restricted diet, you could add one teaspoon of sugar to a large pot of beans or greens and add only fifteen calories to the whole pot. Mother also used pork sowbelly to season most vegetables. Don't do it. We will find various substitutes, and no one will be the wiser—just thinner.

Always keep homemade fat-free chicken stock on hand for cooking vegetables such as greens, squash, green beans, and peas. See under "Entrees—Chicken" for homemade chicken stock.

Mother always cooked a huge pot of collard greens the day after Christmas. She said it would clean out our systems after all that rich food on Christmas Day. Mama's collard greens were not without fat, however, what with all that sowbelly she used for seasoning. We will use bacon bits (imitation) or homemade chicken stock for our after-Christmas collards. We can have a whole cupful for only 65 calories. Add one corn muffin and a couple of wedges of pickled beets, and that will make a fine lunch.

A cupful of spinach has only 40 calories. If you want to cut calories, you can have turnip greens for only 30 calories. Fresh kale has only 45 calories per cupful, but who wants to rob their winter flower bed of the beautiful white and green or purple and green curly kale leaves, for Pete's sake! Last year I got on the kale kick and set out plants in my Mexican flower pots. They were so gorgeous with the magenta grey-green leaves glistening in the winter sun, casting intricate patterned shadows onto each other . . . no way I could have put this handsome work of art in a stew pot.

But there is a place for everything. My beautiful kale plants, until recently considered only a vegetable, are still relegated to the back yard even in their Mexican flower pots. However, on a recent trip to New York City, I was startled to see the once lowly kale plant in a flower box in front of a Fifth Avenue skyscraper. The next thing you know, they'll be raising collards in front of the colosseum and turnips in the Trump Tower.

———— Baked Acorn Squash #1 ————

2 acorn squash
1/2 tsp. brown sugar substitute
4 tsp. low-fat margarine
Dash of salt

Cut acorn squash in half lengthwise. Place cut side down on baking dish. Bake in 350° oven for 25 minutes, or until tender. Turn the squash halves upright. Sprinkle 1/2 tsp. of brown sugar substitute on each half. Coat each half with 1 tsp. of low-fat margarine. Return to oven and cook for 10 or 15 minutes.

4 Servings: 74 Calories per Serving; 2 grams Fat; 0 Cholesterol; 0.3 grams Saturated Fat.

Food Exchanges: 1 bread.

Baked Acorn Squash #2

I saw a real neat idea recently in a newspaper food section about acorn squash as a holiday dish. Cut one acorn squash into four pieces across the grain (this would resemble a pineapple slice). Put in a flat baking pan with foil laid over lightly. Bake for about 15 minutes. Take foil off; sprinkle margarine and sugar substitute on top and bake uncovered for about 15 minutes. You could divide a 1/2 oz. packet of raisins among the four slices, which would increase the calories by only ten per serving. Prepared this way, each serving would be 1/4 of the squash, instead of 1/2 as in #1, and with raisins the total calorie count is 67.

Baked Corn

1 can creamed corn (17 oz.) or 2 cups stewed
   fresh corn
1/4 cup frozen egg substitute, thawed
2 tsp. sugar
1 tsp. cornstarch
1/4 cup skim milk
1/4 tsp. nutmeg
Salt and pepper to taste

Mix all ingredients well except nutmeg. Pour into a casserole baking dish which has been sprayed with a vegetable spray. Sprinkle nutmeg on top. Bake in 350° oven for 45 to 55 minutes.

4 Servings: 131 Calories per Serving; 2 grams Fat; 1 mg. Cholesterol; 0.4 grams Saturated Fat.

Food Exchanges: 1-1/2 bread.

Barbecued Green Beans

I found the original recipe for this dish at our Art League's potluck Christmas dinner party. My artist friends would recognize the difference in ingredients, but they would not likely recognize a difference in taste. This would be great for the Fourth of July cookout instead of the usual baked beans.

> 2 cans (16 oz.) green beans, French cut
> 1 small onion (2/3 cup) chopped
> 2/3 cup Weight Watchers ketchup
> 1/4 cup brown sugar
> 1 tsp. Sweet'n Low brown sugar
> 2 Tbs. bacon bits (imitation)

Drain beans. Sauté onion in nonstick frypan which has been coated with vegetable cooking spray. Mix all other ingredients together. Put beans and onion in casserole baking pan. Pour remaining ingredients over. Cover lightly with foil. Bake in 300° oven for about 2 hours.

8 Servings: 71 Calories per Serving; 0 Fat; 0 Cholesterol; 0 Saturated Fat.

Food Exchanges: 1 vegetable; 1 fat.

Broccoli Casserole

1 small onion
1/2 cup celery, chopped
1 Tbs. low-fat margarine
1 cup cooked broccoli
1/2 cup water
1/2 cup grated cheddar cheese (2 oz.) Light (90
   cal. per oz.)
1/4 cup mushrooms
1 cup skim milk
1 Tbs. flour
1 cup cooked rice

Sauté onion, celery, and mushrooms in melted margarine. Add cooked chopped broccoli. Mix flour with skim milk and add to vegetables. Add to rice, and stir until well blended. Place in casserole baking dish that has been sprayed with vegetable spray. Cover lightly and bake at 350° about 35 to 40 minutes.

6 Servings: 99 Calories per Serving; 2 grams Fat; 4 mg. Cholesterol; 1 gram Saturated Fat.

Food Exchanges: 1 bread; 1 vegetable.

Eggplant Casserole

I had collected three very similar recipes for eggplant casserole and wanted to try them again to decide which one to
include in this book. I wanted a recipe which might substitute
for dressing with turkey or chicken. My deadline was pressing
down on me, but there were no eggplants in my supermarket.
I called around town and talked to the produce managers.
Finally I located some—the manager said he had a few, but
they were very expensive, due to the Texas Valley and Florida
freeze. When my husband went to pick one up, the produce
manager said he was embarrassed to tell him the price—
$2.98 for one eggplant! I just wanted you to know the price
I paid to give you the very best eggplant casserole that I could
come up with.

> 1 eggplant
> 4 slices white bread (40 calories per slice)
> 1/2 cup canned evaporated skim milk
> 1 Tbs. low-fat margarine
> 1/4 cup onion, finely chopped
> 1/2 cup celery, finely chopped
> 1/2 cup egg substitute
> 1 Tbs. pimiento, chopped
> 1/2 tsp. salt
> 1/2 tsp. pepper
> 1/2 tsp. sage
> 1/2 tsp. paprika
> 1 cup grated cheddar cheese, light

Peel eggplant. Cut into one-inch cubes and soak in lightly
salted water for one or two hours. Rinse and drain. Cover with water

in a saucepan and cook over medium heat until tender. Drain. Soak bread cubes in canned skim milk.

Sauté onions and celery in melted margarine until onions are translucent. Combine cooked eggplant, bread cubes, sautéed vegetables, grated cheese, salt, pepper, and sage. Add egg substitute and pimiento. Blend thoroughly. Pour into casserole baking dish which has been sprayed with vegetable cooking spray. Sprinkle paprika over top. Bake at 350° for 45 minutes.

8 Servings: 122 Calories per Serving; 5 grams Fat; 7 mg. Cholesterol; 1 gram Saturated Fat.

Food Exchanges: 1/2 meat; 1/2 bread; 1/2 vegetable; 1 fat.

Mrs. McMullan's Extra Good
————— Squash Casserole —————

I found this recipe, yellowed from age, in Deenie's recipe box. It brought back waves of nostalgia, as I remembered the many happy hours I spent at the McMullan's house visiting Kitty, her daughter and my best friend. Mrs. M. would have been surprised and a little sceptical if she could have known how good her recipe turned out without her fresh country eggs, whole milk, and country butter.

5 or 6 medium yellow squash
1 medium onion
2 garlic cloves
1/4 lb. cheddar cheese, light, grated
8 soda crackers, crumbled
1/4 cup egg substitute
1/2 cup skim milk
Salt and pepper to taste
1/2 tsp. paprika

Cut up squash and parboil until tender. Sauté onion and garlic in nonstick skillet. Drain squash and mash.

Spray a casserole baking dish with vegetable cooking spray. Place a layer of one half of the squash on bottom, then a layer of crumbled soda crackers, then a layer of grated cheese. Beat milk and egg substitute. Pour one half of the milk–egg mixture over the top. Repeat a second layer, with milk–egg mixture on top. Sprinkle with paprika.

8 Servings; 96 Calories per Serving; 4 grams Fat; 7 mg. Cholesterol; 1.6 grams Saturated Fat.

Food Exchanges: 1 meat; 1 vegetable; 1/2 fat.

—— Spaghetti Squash Casserole ——

3 cups spaghetti squash, cooked
1/2 cup egg substitute
1/4 cup bell pepper, chopped
1/3 cup onion, chopped
1/4 cup water chestnuts
1 Tbs. pimiento
1/2 cup artificial sour cream
1/2 cup skim milk
1/2 cup cheese, grated (light cheddar)
1/2 tsp. pepper
1/2 tsp. salt
1 tsp. paprika

In case you have not tried spaghetti squash, I urge you to do so. It is usually found with the exotic food in the produce section of the supermarket.

Cut the squash lengthwise. Place cut-side down on a cookie sheet and bake in oven at 350° for 25 minutes. When it is done, take a fork and scoop out the meat of the squash. It will look like boiled yellow spaghetti—thus the name. Since this makes a large amount, you may want to freeze half of it to serve as a side dish at a later date, or make another casserole.

For the Casserole: Mix spaghetti squash, onion, bell pepper, water chestnuts, pimiento, cheese, pepper and salt. Add egg substitute. Mix artificial sour cream and skim milk together, and fold into mixture. Pour into a 6x10″ casserole dish sprayed with vegetable cooking spray. Sprinkle paprika on the top. Bake in 350° oven for 35 minutes.

This is really company fare, and no one, I repeat *no one* will suspect that this is a low-calorie dish.

Note. Cubes of jicama sautéed with water in a Teflon skillet can be substituted for water chestnuts. There is not enough difference in calories to count.

8 Servings: 112 Calories per Serving; 5 grams Fat; 4 mg. Cholesterol; 3 grams Saturated Fat.

Food Exchanges: 1 meat; 1 fat.

Fried Potatoes

Ten years ago when we wrote down my mother's Depression days' recipes, we told you two ways in which she fried potatoes. We did not include French fries because my mother did not make French fries. She was too saving of the yearly supply of lard to use a whole skilletful for a few potatoes. When that was gone, there wasn't going to be anymore until next fall's hog killing. Mother had never heard of cholesterol, and I don't think anyone else had either, except perhaps the scientists. I know that the first time I ever heard of cholesterol was in 1948, and it was spelled "Kolestral", supposedly came from sheep oil, and was used as an oil treatment for split-ended hair.

In the recipes for fried potatoes which I gave you in the earlier book, I suggested that you might use lard, Crisco, oil, or bacon grease. Now I am recommending none of the above except cholesterol-free vegetable oil or olive oil. How about trying the following recipe:

Microwave "Fried Potatoes"

Select four medium-size red-skinned potatoes. Wash, but do not peel. Slice across the grain in about 1/4-inch slices. Place in the bottom of a microwave-safe baking dish which has been coated with a vegetable cooking spray. Sprinkle about one teaspoon of Molly McButter and one tablespoon of Parmesan cheese over all the potato slices. Bake on high for about two minutes, or however long it takes potatoes to be tender. If you do not care for the cheese, substitute a sprinkle of paprika. These potatoes are pleasing to the eye as well as to the palate.

4 Servings: 128 Calories per Serving; 1 gram Fat; 1 mg. Cholesterol; 0.3 grams Saturated Fat.

Food Exchanges: 1-1/2 bread.

Pan-Fried Potatoes

Wash and peel four medium-size potatoes. Pat dry. Slice across the grain in about 1/8-inch slices. Sprinkle with salt—very little, mind you. Cover the bottom of a Teflon skillet with 2 teaspoons of oil. Brown the potatoes to a very light brown, and turn. Add one half of a medium onion, if desired. After the potatoes have been lightly browned on both sides, add about one-half cup of water. Cover tightly, and lower the heat. Stir occasionally and let cook for about twenty minutes. Add additional water if necessary. This is an excellent way to fry potatoes on a camping or hunting trip.

4 Servings: 147 Calories per Serving; 3 grams Fat; 1 mg. Cholesterol; 0.6 grams Saturated Fat.

Food Exchanges: 1-1/2 bread; 1/2 fat.

──────────── Goulash ────────────

1 tsp. vegetable oil
1 cup onions, chopped
3/4 cup green pepper, chopped
4 medium tomatoes, peeled and quartered
2 cups fresh okra, sliced
1/4 tsp. salt
1/2 tsp. pepper

Coat a nonstick skillet with vegetable cooking spray. Add oil. Sauté onion and green pepper until tender. Add tomatoes, okra, and seasoning. Add 1/2 cup of water. Cover and cook for seven to ten minutes, stirring occasionally.

7 Servings: 44 Calories per Serving; 1 gram Fat; 0 Cholesterol; 0.14 grams Saturated Fat.

Food Exchanges: 2 vegetable.

Macaroni and Cheese

Although Macaroni and Cheese may be used as an entree, it is more often used as a side dish. Therefore, we are including it in this chapter.

1 cup elbow macaroni, uncooked (2 cups cooked)
1 Tbs. flour
1 Tbs. low-fat margarine
1/4 tsp. salt
1/4 tsp. pepper
1-1/2 cups skim milk
1 cup grated Cheddar cheese (reduced fat to 1/3)
Paprika

Cook macaroni according to package directions. Drain. In a saucepan, blend margarine and flour. Add salt and pepper. Add skim milk gradually and cook until mixture is smooth and heated through. Stir in grated cheese. Mix sauce with macaroni. Place in casserole dish which has been sprayed with vegetable cooking spray. Sprinkle with paprika. Bake in moderate oven (350°) until thoroughly heated through and browned on top—about 30 minutes. If you would like to add a zingy taste to this, add one tablespoon of Worcestershire sauce before baking.

6 Servings: 116 Calories per Serving; 3 grams Fat; 8 mg. Cholesterol; 1.7 grams Saturated Fat.

Food Exchanges: 1/2 meat; 1 bread.

Pickled Beets

I have tried to can pickled beets by cutting down on the sugar and using a sugar substitute, but it has not been very successful. I usually end up throwing them out because they do not look as bright and fresh as I think they should, and I am paranoid about food poisoning with home-canned vegetables without sufficient sugar or salt. I came by this trait honestly. My father stood guard between Mama's canned food and the health of his family. If something didn't look or smell just right, out it went. I'm afraid that the kids took advantage of Dad's watchfulness. When there was something on our plate we did not like, we sniffed suspiciously and wondered if it were spoiled. That was all it took. Everyone at the table had to discard the suspicious food. Wonder of wonders, with lack of adequate refrigeration, and no running water, it now seems to me a miracle that no one in our family ever had food poisoning.

1 can (15-1/2 oz.) of beets
3 pkts. of Sweet'n Low
1/2 cup vinegar
8 cloves
1 stick cinnamon

Place the canned beets and the liquid in a pot. Add 1/2 cup of vinegar, 3 pkts. of Sweet'n Low, cloves, and cinnamon stick. Bring to a boil. Lower the heat and cook for 15 minutes. Cool. Place in a jar, and store in the refrigerator. This will keep for two or three weeks. If you boil a big pot of collards, turnip greens, or pinto beans, and make a pan of cornbread, the beets will be all gone in a day or two.

4 Servings: 43 Calories per Serving; 0 Fat; 0 Cholesterol;
0 Saturated Fat.
Food Exchanges: 2 vegetable.

Pinto Beans

Pinto beans are considered Western, Southern, or Mexican food. In some stores up North, they are known as "migrant beans." Southern, Western, Mexican, whatever, this is a wonderful dish, and no one will miss the sowbelly that my mother put in the pinto bean pot.

When I lived on the Texas-Mexican border, I quickly adopted the habit of serving pinto beans with company meals. I usually served them in individual bean bowls as a replacement for soup at the beginning of the meal, and there I always put chili pequins in my beans. These are little red berries about the size of peppercorns, and grow wild on small gangly bushes. They are so hot that they make jalapeños seem bland. I usually put about five of those little hot demons in a large pot of beans (twice this recipe). It was my own perverted way of playing Russian roulette to see whose bowl the chili pequins would land in.

Most people on the Mexican border put cilantro in pinto beans. Try it, you may like it. I don't.

> 1/2 lb. pinto beans
> 6 cups water
> 1/2 medium onion, chopped
> 1/2 medium bell pepper, chopped
> 1 clove of garlic
> 1 cup of canned tomatoes—or fresh tomatoes, if
>   plentiful
> 1/2 tsp. salt
> 1/4 tsp. celery salt
> 1 tsp. of chili powder, or 3 chili pequins
> 1 pkt. sugar substitute

Pour the beans into a bowl and check over for little rocks or shrivelled-up beans. Wash beans. Put them in a three-quart pot with 6 cups of water. I usually let them soak overnight, although this is not absolutely necessary. The following morning, add all other ingredients, and cook covered for about three hours. About thirty minutes before they are completely done, take out a half cupful of beans and squash them up with a fork. Return to the pot. This will thicken the broth.

(At first you will think that we made a typographical error in writing 6 cups of water. Believe me, the beans will soak the water up.)

In many food plans, pinto beans can be counted as a meat substitute. If you count it as a vegetable, use one-half cup servings.

10 Servings: 110 Calories per Serving; 0 Fat; 0 Cholesterol; 0 Saturated Fat.

Food Exchanges: 1 bread; 1 vegetable.

───── Spicy Black-Eyed Peas ─────

Everyone down South knows that you must eat black-eyed peas on New Year's Day to bring good luck throughout the year. This recipe is designed to help our newcomers to the area, who never had the privilege of being "raised on black-eyed peas and cornbread."

We thought if we doctored the black-eyed peas a bit and put a little zing in them, you would at least eat them on New Year's Day. We know what you say about our unofficial state legume, but do me a favor and try them next New Year's. Heaven knows, we need all the luck we can get. As for me, I'll probably have black-eyed peas, plain vanilla, with canned tomatoes poured over them, and some good ol' cornbread on the side.

2 cans (15 oz.) black-eyed peas, dried
2 tsp. vegetable oil
2 Tbs. bacon bits, imitation
1 can (16 oz.) whole tomatoes
1 cup onion, chopped
1 green pepper, chopped
1 clove garlic
1 tsp. cumin
1 tsp. dry mustard
1/4 tsp. curry powder
1/2 tsp. chili powder
Salt
Pepper

Sauté onion and green pepper in nonstick skillet with 2 teaspoons of vegetable oil. Add black-eyed peas, tomatoes, and seasonings. Bring to a boil. Reduce heat and simmer for twenty minutes. When ready to serve, sprinkle bacon bits on top.

10 Servings: 104 Calories per Serving; 2 Fat; 0 Cholesterol; 0.25 grams Saturated Fat.

Food Exchanges: 1 bread; 1/2 vegetable.

Spinach Crepes

Basic Crepe Recipe

1 cup flour
1/2 cup skim milk
1/2 cup egg substitute
1/2 cup water

1/4 tsp. salt
2 Tbs. low-fat margarine

Place ingredients in blender in order named. Blend at high speed for 30 seconds. Scrape down sides. Blend another 60 seconds until smooth. Let mixture cool in refrigerator for at least two hours. Mixture will keep in refrigerator for two or three days. Cook crepes according to directions on your crepe maker. Crepes can be put between sheets of wax paper and kept in the freezer for a few weeks, when necessary; when ready to use, let them thaw at room temperature for a few minutes.

Filling for Spinach Crepes

For 12 Crepes:

1 (10 oz.) package of frozen chopped spinach, or
   one package of fresh spinach
1 Tbs. low-fat margarine
2 Tbs. flour
1 cup skim milk
1/4 tsp. salt
1/8 tsp. nutmeg
1/8 tsp. pepper
1 cup Swiss cheese
1 Tbs. grated onion
2 Tbs. Parmesan cheese, grated

Cook spinach and drain well; set aside. Melt margarine in saucepan. Add flour and stir until well mixed. Add milk. Stir continuously until sauce is smooth and thickened. To the sauce add salt, nutmeg, pepper, cheese, onion, and spinach. Blend well. When cheese is melted, remove from heat.

On each crepe, brown side down, place one heaping tablespoon of spinach filling. Roll and place seam-side down in baking dish sprayed with vegetable cooking spray. Sprinkle with Parmesan cheese. Bake in pre-heated 375° oven for 15 to 20 minutes.

12 Crepes: 84 Calories per Crepe; 5 grams Fat; 14 mg. Cholesterol; 3 grams Saturated Fat.

Food Exchanges: 1 meat; 1 fat.

Sweet Potato Soufflé

1 cup mashed sweet potatoes (about 3 medium-
*   size potatoes)*
1/4 tsp. salt
1/4 tsp. nutmeg
3 Tbs. flour
1 Tbs. Butter Buds
1/2 cup skim milk
1/4 cup frozen egg substitute
3 egg whites
1 Tbs. sugar
2 pkts. Sweet'n Low

Boil potatoes with skins on. Potatoes are done when you can stick a fork through the middle of them. Cool, and peel off skins. Mash with a potato masher, then beat with an electric beater. Mix salt, nutmeg, and sugar with potatoes. In a small saucepan, dissolve flour and Butter Buds with milk. Heat until mixture begins to thicken. Stir into sweet potatoes, blending well. Add egg substitute to sweet potato mixture, stirring constantly. Beat egg whites until stiff. Carefully fold into potato mixture. Turn into ungreased 1-1/2 quart baking dish. Bake in 350° oven about 1-1/4 hours, or until firm to the touch.

4 Servings: 171 Calories per Serving; 2 grams Fat; 2 mg. Cholesterol; 0.6 grams Saturated Fat.

Food Exchanges: 1 meat; 1-1/2 bread.

── Vegetables in Creamy Herb Sauce ──

This creamy herb sauce can be used to serve over other vegetables, such as cauliflower, new potatoes, and baked onions.

1 cup sliced mushrooms
1/2 cup chopped onions
1 clove garlic, crushed
1/2 tsp. thyme
1/2 tsp. marjoram 1/4 tsp. tarragon
1/4 tsp. pepper
1 can (12 oz.) Weight Watchers mushroom soup
1 cup carrots, scraped and sliced
1/2 bunch broccoli, chopped (about 3 cups)

Steam or boil carrots and broccoli separately and keep warm.

Sauté onions and mushrooms in nonstick skillet sprayed with vegetable cooking spray. Add garlic and spices. Stir in mushroom soup and simmer for five minutes, or until piping hot. Place broccoli and carrots on platter, and pour sauce over.

4 Servings: 77 Calories per Serving; 1 gram Fat; 0 Cholesterol; 0.9 grams Saturated Fat.

Food Exchanges: 2 vegetable.

——————— Yellow Squash ———————

4 medium yellow squash
1 clove garlic
1 can homemade chicken broth, with all fat
    skimmed off
1/2 pkt. Sweet'n Low
1 tsp. low-fat margarine
1/4 tsp. salt
Pepper, to taste

If squash is young and tender, simply cut into one-inch slices crosswise. If the squash is more mature, you will want to peel it. Place in pot. Add heated chicken broth, garlic, Sweet'n Low, and salt and pepper, if desired. Cook on medium heat until tender, and until most liquid has evaporated. I prefer to mash the squash lightly. Add 1 tsp. low-fat margarine (you may substitute Molly McButter).

Serves 2: 66 Calories per Serving; 2 Fat; 0 Cholesterol; 0.2 grams Saturated Fat.

Food Exchanges: 2 vegetable.

Breads

BREADS

I have gathered together several bread recipes which you are going to love to make and love to eat. Before I share them with you, you will have to promise me that for ordinary bread you will buy the "lite" bread—forty calories per slice. Then once per day you can treat yourself to the special homemade breads, providing you limit yourself to one slice, one muffin, one roll, or one serving of pancakes. I have extracted as many calories as possible from the breads, but with flour containing from 400 to 420 calories per cup, and corn meal containing from 435 to 500 calories, there are a lot of calories in bread any way you slice it.

Even though we have cut down on the fat and sugar and are using skim milk and egg substitutes, we've come up with some of the most mouth-watering breads you ever tasted.

While your bread is in the oven emitting that baking bread aroma, best you set your oven timer, synchronize the time with your watch, and get out of there. Go for a walk. Water the plants. Play ball with your kid. Stay as far as possible from the wonderful aroma which permeates every nook and cranny of your house.

When you take the bread out of the oven, place the loaf on a rack, cover it with a cup towel, and get back out of there. Do not try to slice the bread while it is hot. Two reasons: You cannot slice it thin enough while it is hot, and, you will be too tempted to tear off a hunk and eat it on the spot.

Jail House Rolls

This recipe was given to me by the High Sheriff of Amarillo, Texas, in 1946, just before I was to be married to Troy Dillow, recently returned from Italy with the United States Air Force. At that time my cooking had consisted of opening an occasional can of sardines or Vienna sausage. During World War II, rental housing in Texas was pretty scarce, what with some sort of military establishment in every town. As a single social worker, I was lucky to rent a garage, recently converted into two efficiency apartments, each with a dinky refrigerator, a hot plate, and a roll-away bed. I sent my wartime food ration coupons home to my mother, who desperately needed them to buy sugar and other ingredients for canning. I ate my meals at restaurants where they served "blue plate specials" for fifty cents.

The High Sheriff felt sorry for the three single female social workers officing on the second floor of the courthouse, and whose boyfriends were off somewhere else defending our country. He dropped by every few days for a chat. Occasionally he brought us leftover hot rolls from the jail kitchen. When I left Amarillo, he gave me the recipe for those delicious hot rolls.

These are the rolls I made for my family for thirty years, before it became too tempting to buy brown-and-serves at the supermarket.

I have tampered with the High Sheriff's recipe—have taken out substantial amounts of sugar and substituted vegetable oil for the shortening. The mashed potatoes have remained, because they accounted for the hearty distinctive taste and texture of the rolls.

Jail House Icebox Rolls

I pkg. dry yeast
1/2 cup lukewarm water
1/4 cup vegetable oil
1/4 cup sugar
1/2 tsp. Sweet'n Low
I cup mashed potatoes
I cup skim milk
1/2 cup frozen egg substitute
I tsp. salt
6 cups flour

Boil the peeled and cut-up Irish potatoes in water until tender. Pour off all water. Mash the potatoes, then beat with electric beater. Dissolve yeast in lukewarm water. Scald one cup of skim milk. Add vegetable oil, sugar, sugar substitute, salt, and mashed potatoes to scalded milk. When mixture is cool, add yeast in water, and thawed egg substitute.

To this mixture, gradually add about 4-1/2 cups of flour until well mixed. Place on floured pastry board and knead remaining flour into dough. The secret of these rolls lies in "working the dough." Place dough in large bowl. Spray ever so lightly with vegetable cooking spray to prevent a hard crust from forming on the dough. Cover with a cloth. Set aside in a dry warm place. Let the dough rise to about 2-1/2 times its original size (about 2 or 3 hours). Knead dough again, cover with foil wrap, and let stay in the icebox at least overnight. [You can tell how old this recipe is when the refrigerator is referred to as an icebox.] The dough will keep in the icebox for about a week.

About two hours before baking, make up however many rolls you wish to serve by pinching off pieces about the size of a small unbaked biscuit. Place in a pan or muffin tin which has been sprayed with vegetable cooking spray. Cover with a cloth and put in a dry warm place to rise. Rolls should rise to double or triple their size. Bake in pre-heated 350° oven for about 18 minutes until golden brown. (Sometimes I jazz up mine by inverting the unbaked rolls in a saucer of sesame seeds—one fourth tsp. per roll, adding 4 calories per roll.)

Makes 36 rolls: 102 Calories per roll; 2 grams Fat; 0.3 mg. Cholesterol; 0.3 grams Saturated Fat.

Food Exchanges: 1 bread; 1/2 fat.

Buttermilk Biscuits

2 cups flour
1 Tbs. low-fat margarine
3 tsp. baking powder
1 tsp. baking soda
1/2 tsp. salt
1-1/8 cups buttermilk

Put the baking soda into the buttermilk and set aside. Combine all other dry ingredients. Cut in margarine with pastry cutter. Add buttermilk and stir quickly with a fork, just enough to hold the dough together. Turn out on floured pastry board. Pat down to about 5/8 inch. Cut biscuits with biscuit cutter. Place in baking tin which has been sprayed with vegetable cooking spray. Take a little skim milk, and with a spoon or pastry brush, lightly coat the top of each biscuit with milk. This will help in browning evenly. My mother deftly handled the biscuit dough, rolling out each biscuit without a cutter. But then, she made biscuits, two dozen of them, every morning for breakfast. I was going to suggest that if you do not have a biscuit cutter, a Vienna sausage tin would do, but they now come with a lift-up lid and are thereby unsuitable as a cutter. The nearest thing which I found in my pantry is a can of tomato paste—that will make a two-inch cutter.

16 two-inch Biscuits: 68 Calories per Biscuit; 1 gram Fat; 1 mg. Cholesterol; 0.2 grams Saturated Fat.

Food Exchanges: 1 bread.

Butterflake Biscuits

1 cup all-purpose flour
3 tsp. baking powder
1/4 tsp. salt
2 Tbs. margarine
1 Tbs. Butter Buds, dry
1/8 cup egg substitute
1 egg white
1/6 cup cold skim milk
1/3 cup flour, for pastry board

Sift dry ingredients together. Cut margarine into mixture with pastry blender. Beat egg white and egg substitute. Add milk to eggs and beat well. Add eggs and milk to dry ingredients and mix lightly with a fork. Shape into a ball and place on a floured pastry board. Spread dough into a rectangle shape and press down to 1/2-inch thickness. Fold one end over. Press down again to 1/2-inch thickness. Use a 2-inch biscuit cutter to cut 8 biscuits. Place biscuits in baking pan that has been sprayed with vegetable cooking spray and bake in pre-heated 450° oven for fifteen minutes.

The secret in biscuit-making is to handle the dough very gently, both in mixing and in rolling it out.

8 Biscuits: 106 Calories per Biscuit; 2 grams Fat; 0 Cholesterol; 0.4 grams Saturated Fat.

Food Exchanges: 1 bread; 1/2 fat.

Cornbread Muffins

1 cup corn meal
1 cup flour
3 tsp. baking powder
1/2 tsp. salt
2 Tbs. vegetable oil
1 pkt. sweetener
1-1/4 cup skim milk
1/4 cup egg substitute

Mix flour, meal, baking powder, salt, and sweetener together. Beat oil and egg substitute together. Add milk. Gradually add flour–meal mixture to milk–egg mixture, using an electric beater, and beat thoroughly. It is better to let batter sit for about five minutes before putting in muffin pans.

Coat muffin tins with vegetable cooking spray; fill to one half full. Bake in pre-heated 400° oven for about 15 to 17 minutes.

12 Muffins: 117 Calories per Muffin; 2 grams Fat; 0.5 mg. Cholesterol; 0 Saturated Fat.

Food Exchanges: 1 bread; 1/2 fat.

Country Cornbread

1 cup cornmeal
3/4 cup flour
1 Tbs. sugar
1/4 tsp. Sweet'n Low
1 tsp. salt
4 tsp. baking powder
1/2 tsp. baking soda
1/2 cup egg substitute
1 cup low-cal buttermilk
2 Tbs. vegetable cooking oil

Stir baking soda into buttermilk and set aside. Mix dry ingredients. Add buttermilk, oil, egg substitute to dry ingredients and beat with an electric beater or hand mixer for about two minutes. Pour into an iron skillet, which has been coated with vegetable cooking spray. Bake in pre-heated 400° oven for about 18 minutes until golden brown. (You don't really have to have an iron skillet. Any bread pan will do).

12 Servings: 120 Calories per Serving; 4 grams Fat; 1 mg. Cholesterol; 1 gram Saturated Fat.

Food Exchanges: 1 bread; 1 fat.

You may bake this in a 12-muffin pan. Bake 15 to 17 minutes.

12 muffins: 130 calories per Muffin; 4.5 grams Fat; 1 mg. Cholesterol; 1 gram Saturated Fat.

Food Exchanges: 1 bread; 2/3 fat.

Stone-Ground Cornbread

1-1/2 cups stone-ground cornmeal
1/2 cup flour
1 tsp. baking powder
1 tsp. baking soda
Salt
1/4 cup frozen egg substitute, thawed
2 cups low-cal buttermilk
2 Tbs. vegetable cooking oil

Add baking soda to buttermilk, and set aside. Combine cornmeal, flour, baking powder, and salt. Add oil and egg substitute to buttermilk. Combine dry ingredients with liquids. Beat with electric beater until smooth.

Spray a 12-cup muffin tin with vegetable cooking spray. Fill muffin cups about half full. Bake in pre heated 400° oven for 15 to 18 minutes.

12 Muffins: 118 Calories per Muffin; 2 grams Fat; 2 mg. Cholesterol; 0.5 grams Saturated Fat.

Food Exchanges: 1 bread; 1/2 fat.

Oatmeal Pancakes

1-1/2 cups regular oats, uncooked
1/2 cup whole wheat flour
1 tsp. baking soda
1/8 tsp. salt
2 tsp. sugar
2 cups buttermilk
1/2 cup egg substitute
1 tsp. vanilla

Combine first five ingredients. Add buttermilk, egg substitute, and vanilla. Stir well. Cook on nonstick griddle which has been sprayed with vegetable cooking spray.

One pancake makes a rather substantial serving for a weight-conscious person. Non-dieters can have two.

10 Pancakes: 110 Calories per Pancake; 3 grams Fat; 2 mg. Cholesterol; 0.7 grams Saturated Fat.

Food Exchange: 1 bread; 1/2 fat.

Pancakes

1 cup flour
1 Tbs. baking powder
1/4 tsp. salt
2 pkts. Sweet One
1/2 tsp. baking powder
1/4 cup egg substitute
1 cup low-cal buttermilk
2 tsp. Butter Buds
1/3 cup water

Put baking soda in 1 cup of buttermilk. Mix other dry ingredients; add egg substitute and milk. Beat with hand mixer until ingredients are well blended. Add the water gradually until batter is at proper consistency. Spray Teflon griddle or skillet with vegetable cooking spray. Preheat griddle. Use a 1/3 cup measuring cup to ladle the pancake mixture onto the griddle. Brown on one side until bubbles begin to form on top. Turn pancakes over and cook until they are light brown on other side. Stack three pancakes on each plate for a serving. Use "lite" pancake syrup. (Two tablespoons of light syrup equals 50 calories.) If you want a special Sunday breakfast, serve with one turkey sausage patty.

3 Servings, 3 Pancakes per Serving: 135 Calories per Serving; 0 Fat; 0 Cholesterol; 0.7 grams Saturated Fat.

Food Exchanges: 3 pancakes: 1-1/2 breads.

—— Banana Oatmeal Muffins ——

1 cup oatmeal (quick, or old-fashioned, uncooked)
1 cup flour
1/2 tsp. baking soda
1/2 Tbs. baking powder
1 cup skim milk
1/2 cup mashed ripe banana
2 Tbs. vegetable oil
3 pkts. sweetener
1 egg white
1/4 tsp. almond extract

Combine oats, flour, and baking powder. Add remaining ingredients. Stir until dry ingredients are moistened. Spray a 12-cup muffin tin with vegetable cooking spray. Fill prepared muffin cups 3/4 full. Bake in 400° oven for about 17 minutes or until golden brown.

12 Muffins: 104 Calories per Muffin; 3 grams Fat; 0 Cholesterol; 0.4 grams Saturated Fat.

Food Exchanges: 1 bread; 1/2 fat.

— Best Ever Oatmeal Raisin Muffins —

1 cup quick-cooking oatmeal, uncooked
1 cup buttermilk
1/4 cup egg substitute
2 Tbs. brown sugar
1-1/2 tsp. brown sugar substitute
2 Tbs. vegetable oil
1 cup flour
1 tsp. baking powder
1/2 tsp. baking soda
1/2 tsp. salt
1/2 cup raisins

Combine oatmeal and buttermilk in large mixing bowl. Let stand one hour. Add egg substitute, sugar, sweetener, and oil, stirring well. Combine remaining ingredients, except raisins, in a medium bowl. Add to oatmeal mixture, stirring just to moisten. Stir in raisins.

Spray muffin tins with vegetable cooking spray. Spoon mixture into muffin tins. Bake in pre-heated 400° oven for 18 minutes.

18 Muffins: 81 calories per Muffin; 2 grams Fat; 0 Cholesterol; 0.4 grams Saturated Fat.

Food Exchanges: 1 bread.

——————— Bran Muffins ———————

1 cup bran
1 Tbs. sugar
2 tsp. baking powder
6 Tbs. water
6 Tbs. powdered nonfat milk
1/4 cup egg substitute

1 medium apple, chopped
1/2 tsp. sweetener
1/2 tsp. cinnamon
1/4 tsp. nutmeg
1/2 tsp. vanilla extract
5 drops almond extract

Place egg substitute, water, powdered milk, sweetener, baking powder, spices, and flavoring in electric blender. Blend on high for 30 seconds; drop apple chunks in and chop for 20 seconds. Pour in bowl. Stir in bran. Pour batter into an 8-cup muffin tin, which has been sprayed with vegetable cooking spray. Bake in pre-heated 350° oven for 25 minutes.

8 Muffins: 58 Calories per Muffin; 1 gram fat; 1 mg. Cholesterol; 0 Saturated Fat.

Food Exchanges: 1/2 bread.

Blueberry Bran Muffins

10 Tbs. bran
3 Tbs. flour
5 Tbs. water
5 Tbs. powdered skim milk
1/4 cup frozen egg substitute
1/3 cup blueberries
2 Tbs. sugar
3 pkts. sweetener
1/2 tsp. cinnamon
1/2 tsp. nutmeg
1/2 tsp. vanilla
1/4 tsp. almond extract

Mix dry ingredients. Beat egg substitute with water. Blend into dry ingredients. Add vanilla and almond extract. Spray 6-cup muffin tin with vegetable cooking spray. Bake in preheated 350° oven 22–25 minutes.

6 Muffins: 71 Calories per Muffin; 2 grams Fat; 1 mg. Cholesterol; 0 Saturated Fat.

Food Exchanges: 1 bread.

—— Carrots–Oat Bran Muffins ——

1-1/4 cups oat bran
3/4 cup flour
2 Tbs. brown sugar
1/2 tsp. brown sugar substitute
2 tsp. baking powder
1 tsp. ground cinnamon
1/4 tsp. salt
1/4 cup raisins
2 egg whites, slightly beaten
3/4 cup skim milk
2 Tbs. honey
2 Tbs. vegetable oil
1 cup shredded carrots

In a large mixing bowl, combine oat bran, flour, brown sugar, sweetener, baking powder, cinnamon, salt, and raisins. Set aside.

In a small bowl, combine egg whites, milk, honey, oil, and carrots, blending well with a fork. Add egg–milk mixture to dry ingredients, and stir just until dry ingredients are moistened. Spray a 12-cup muffin tin, preferably nonstick, with vegetable cooking spray. Spoon batter into cups, each 3/4 full. Bake in pre-heated 400° oven for 20 to 22 minutes, or until golden brown.

12 Muffins: 119 Calories per Muffin; 3 grams Fat; 0 Cholesterol; 0 Saturated Fat.

Food Exchanges: 1 bread; 1/2 fat.

———— Honey Oatmeal Muffins ————

1 cup oatmeal, quick-cooking
3/4 cup flour
3/4 cup whole wheat flour
3 tsp. baking powder
1/8 tsp. salt
1/8 cup egg substitute
3 Tbs. honey
1 Tbs. vegetable oil
1 cup skim milk

Combine all dry ingredients in mixing bowl. Make a well in center of mixture and set aside. Combine egg substitute, honey, oil, and milk. Mix well. Add liquid mixture to dry ingredients. Stir just enough to moisten. Spoon into muffin tin which has been sprayed with vegetable cooking spray. Bake in pre-heated 350° oven for 18 minutes.

12 Muffins: 118 Calories per Muffin; 2 grams Fat; 0 Cholesterol; 0 Saturated Fat.

Food Exchanges: 1 bread; 1/2 fat.

——— Oatmeal–Molasses Muffins ———

2 cups flour
2 Tbs. sugar
1 pkt. sweetener
3 tsp. baking powder
1/2 tsp. salt
1 cup quick-cooking oatmeal
2 egg whites
3/4 cup skim milk
2 Tbs. vegetable cooking oil
1/4 cup molasses

Sift flour, baking powder, salt, and sugars into medium-size bowl. Stir in oatmeal. Combine egg whites, slightly beaten, with milk, vegetable oil, and molasses in small bowl and add all at once to dry ingredients. Stir until moist, but do not over mix.

Spray muffin pan with vegetable cooking spray. Spoon 1/3 cup batter into 18 muffin cups. Bake in pre-heated 400° oven 20 minutes or until golden brown. Remove from pan at once.

18 Muffins: 104 Calories per Muffin; 2 grams Fat; 0 Cholesterol; 0 Saturated Fat.

Food Exchanges: 1 bread; 1/2 fat.

—————— Pumpkin–Prune Muffins ——————

2/3 cup nonfat dry milk
1 cup canned pumpkin
3/4 tsp. nutmeg
3/4 tsp. allspice
3/4 tsp. ginger
1 tsp. cinnamon
6 pkts. Sweet One
1 Tbs. sugar
6 Tbs. flour
1 tsp. baking soda
1/2 cup frozen egg substitute
1 tsp. vanilla
4 Tbs. chopped prunes, uncooked
1/2 cup grated carrots

Combine all dry ingredients. In another mixing bowl combine egg substitute, vanilla, and pumpkin, and mix well. Add prunes and grated carrots. Slowly stir in dry ingredients. Pour into an 8-muffin pan which has been sprayed with vegetable cooking spray. Bake in preheated oven at 350° for fifteen minutes.

8 Muffins: 101 Calories per muffin; 2-1/4 grams Fat; 1-1/2 mg. Cholesterol; 0.6 grams Saturated Fat.

Food Exchanges: 1-1/4 bread.

Banana Bread

I cup whole wheat flour
1/2 cup white flour
2 tsp. baking powder
I tsp. baking soda
1/2 tsp. salt
1/2 cup wheat germ
3 medium, very ripe bananas (one cup mashed)
1/4 cup buttermilk
1/8 vegetable oil
1/4 egg substitute
8 pkts. Sweet One
I Tbs. sugar
I Tbs. Butter Buds
1/2 cup grated carrots

Sift flour, sugar, baking powder, baking soda, and salt. Mix in wheat germ. Add all remaining ingredients and beat until well blended. Place in 8x4" loaf pan that has been sprayed with vegetable cooking spray. Bake in pre-heated oven at 350° for about one hour, or until done. One loaf makes 16 slices.

16 Slices: 104 Calories per Slice; 3 grams Fat; 0 Cholesterol; 0.5 grams Saturated Fat.

Food Exchanges: 1/2 bread; 1/2 fruit; 1/2 fat.

Caraway–Raisin Oat Bread

1/2 cup regular oats, uncooked
I Tbs. low-fat margarine
I cup boiling water

1 pkg. dry yeast
2 Tbs. plus 2 tsp. warm water
1/4 cup honey
1 tsp. salt
1/3 cup raisins
1 tsp. caraway seeds
1-1/2 cups flour
3/4 cup whole wheat flour

Combine oats, margarine, and boiling water in a large bowl. Set aside. Dissolve yeast in the warm water in a small bowl. Let stand five minutes. When oats mixture becomes lukewarm, add honey, salt, and yeast mixture. Mix well. Stir in raisins and caraway seeds. Combine flours, and stir in oats mixture.

Turn dough onto a floured surface, and knead five to eight minutes until smooth and elastic, adding extra flour if needed to keep from sticking. Place in a bowl coated with vegetable cooking spray. Turn over so that top of bread will be coated. Cover with a towel and place in a warm place (85°) to rise for about one hour, or until doubled in size.

Punch dough down. Turn out onto a floured surface, and knead four or five times. Shape dough into a loaf and place in an 8-1/2x4-1/2" loaf pan, which has been coated with vegetable cooking spray. Cover and place in a warm place to rise again for about thirty minutes or until doubled in size. Bake in pre-heated 350° oven for 30 to 35 minutes. Cool on wire rack.

16 Slices: 97 Calories per slice; 1 gram Fat; 0 Cholesterol; 0.13 grams Saturated Fat.

Food Exchanges: 1 bread.

Cranberry Nut Bread

2 cups flour
1/4 cup sugar
6 pkts. sweetener
1-1/2 tsp. baking powder
1/2 tsp. salt
1/2 tsp. baking soda
2 tsp. baking powder
4 Tbs. vegetable oil
1/4 cup frozen egg substitute, thawed
3/4 cup orange juice
1 Tbs. grated orange rind
1 cup cranberries, coarsely chopped
1/4 cup walnuts, chopped
1 Tbs. flour

Sift together 2 cups flour, sugar, and sweetener, baking powder, salt, and baking soda in bowl. Add vegetable oil. Combine egg substitute, orange juice, and orange rind in another small bowl. Add to dry ingredients all at once. Stir just until moistened.

Combine cranberries, walnuts, and 1 Tbs. flour; stir into batter. Pour into 9x5x3" loaf pan which has been sprayed with vegetable cooking spray. Bake in pre-heated 350° oven for one hour, or until bread tests done. Cool in pan on rack 10 minutes. Remove from pan; cool on rack. Makes one loaf.

16 slices: 121 Calories per slice; 5 grams Fat; 0 Cholesterol; 0 Saturated Fat.

Food Exchanges: 1 bread; 1 fruit.

Deenie's Hot Rolls

My sister Deenie couldn't believe her ears when I asked her to make her famous rolls without her favorite vegetable shortening, and with only 2 tablespoons of sugar. She did it anyway because she loves me, and then invited me to lunch to try them. Deenie fretted a bit that the rolls did not quite measure up to her usual "lighter than air, melt in your mouth" standard. They sure tasted good to me . . . all three of them that melted in my mouth.

> 2 cups skim milk, scalded
> 1/4 cup sugar
> 1 pkg. dry yeast
> 2 pkts. sweetener
> 2 Tbs. vegetable oil
> 1 tsp. salt
> 1/2 cup lukewarm water
> 5 cups flour
> 1/2 cup egg substitute

Dissolve dry yeast in 1/2 cup lukewarm water. Heat milk in saucepan to boiling point. Add sugar, sweetener, oil, and salt. Let milk cool to room temperature. Add yeast mixture. Pour into a mixing bowl and add flour a cup at a time. When you have added one cup of flour, add egg substitute and mix well. Continue adding flour, leaving 1/2 cup for the pastry board. When dough is firm, place on pastry board and continue to knead.

Place dough in a large bowl, which has been sprayed with vegetable cooking spray. Cover with a cup towel, and put in a warm dry place to rise. In about two hours, the dough should have doubled in size. Place back on floured board and punch down and spread out to about 3/4-inch thick. Cut with a 1-1/2 inch biscuit cutter. Place rolls in muffin tins, which have been sprayed with vegetable cooking spray. Let rise again to double in size. Bake in pre-heated 375° oven for about 18 minutes. Rolls should be lightly browned when done.

28 Rolls: 79 Calories per Roll; 2 grams Fat; 0.4 Cholesterol; 0.2 Saturated Fat.

Food Exchanges: 1 bread.

——————————— Dilly Bread ———————————

I will only suggest to you the details of the time I doubled this recipe in order to give the additional loaf to my friend Frances, who had raved about my Dilly Bread. I put the double recipe in the same size bowl I had used for a single recipe and put it in my warm oven to rise. Rise it did, up to the top of the bowl, pushing off the cloth, and over the side, through two oven racks, through the heating element, and landed in a large heap on the bottom of the oven, and kept on rising. My friend got her loaf of Dilly Bread. I got a dilly of a mess to clean up.

> *1 pkg. (1 Tbs.) dry yeast*
> *1/4 cup warm water*
> *1 cup cottage cheese (low-fat)*
> *1 Tbs. sugar*
> *1 Tbs. instant minced onions*
> *1-1/2 Tbs. low-fat margarine*
> *2 Tbs. dill seed*
> *1/2 tsp. salt*

1/2 tsp. baking soda
2 egg whites
2-2/3 cups all-purpose flour

Soften yeast in warm water. Heat cottage cheese until luke-warm. Add sugar, onion, margarine, dill seed, salt, baking soda, and egg whites. Mix well. Add softened yeast and flour. Cover and let rise in a warm place until double in size. Knead down and turn into a 9x5″ loaf pan that has been sprayed with vegetable cooking spray, and spray more ever so lightly over top of loaf. Bake in pre-heated 350° oven for 40 to 45 minutes. Makes one loaf.

16 Slices: 96 Calories per Slice; 1 Fat; 0 Cholesterol; 0.2 grams Saturated Fat.

Food Exchanges: 1 bread.

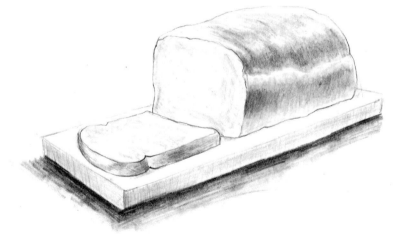

Orange Nut Loaf

2 cups flour
2 tsp. baking powder
1/2 tsp. baking soda
1/2 tsp. salt
1/4 cup walnuts, chopped
1 Tbs. grated orange rind
1/3 cup cut-up prunes
1/4 cup frozen egg substitute, thawed
2 Tbs. sugar
4 pkts. sweetener
2 Tbs. low-fat margarine
1/3 cup orange juice
2/3 cup water
1 tsp. vanilla
1/8 tsp. almond extract

Sift together flour, baking powder, baking soda, and salt. Stir in walnuts, orange rind, and prunes. Combine egg substitute, sugar, sweetener, margarine, orange juice, water, vanilla, and walnut extract. Add dry ingredients all at once; stir just until moistened. Pour into a 8-1/2x4-1/2x2-1/2" loaf pan that has been sprayed with vegetable cooking spray. Bake in a pre-heated 325° oven for 55 minutes, or until bread tests done. Cool in pan on rack 10 minutes. Remove from pan; cool on rack. Makes one loaf.

16 Slices: 87 Calories per Slice; 2 grams Fat; 0 Cholesterol; 0.3 grams Saturated Fat.

Food Exchanges: 1 bread.

Prune Walnut Loaf

2 cups flour
1/2 tsp. salt
1 tsp. baking powder
1 tsp. baking soda
1 cup prunes, uncooked and chopped
1/4 cup walnuts, chopped
2 Tbs. vegetable oil
1 cup boiling water
2 Tbs. sugar
6 pkts. sweetener
1 tsp. vanilla
1/4 cup frozen egg substitute

Sift together flour, salt, baking powder, and baking soda. Combine prunes, walnuts, and oil in a bowl. Add boiling water and beat with a wooden spoon for about a minute. Stir in sugar, vanilla, and egg substitute. Mix well. Add dry ingredients; beat well. Pour into a 9x5x3″ loaf pan which has been sprayed with vegetable cooking spray. Bake in pre-heated 350° oven 45 to 55 minutes, or until bread tests done by inserting a toothpick. Cool in pan on rack 10 minutes. Remove from pan and continue cooling on rack.

16 Slices: 116 Calories per Slice; 3 grams Fat; 0 Cholesterol; 0.4 grams Saturated Fat.

Food Exchanges: 1 bread; 1 fat.

Pumpkin Raisin Bread

1 pkg. dry yeast
1/4 cup warm water
1 cup pumpkin, cooked or canned
1 Tbs. sugar
1 Tbs. margarine
1/2 tsp. baking soda
1/2 tsp. salt
1/4 cup egg substitute
1/2 tsp. Sweet'n Low
3-1/2 cups flour
1/4 cup golden raisins

Dissolve yeast in 1/4 cup of lukewarm water. In a saucepan, heat pumpkin to lukewarm. Add sugar, sweetener, margarine, baking soda, and salt. Mix well. Add egg substitute, and beat with fork or hand mixer for 30 seconds.

Add dissolved yeast to pumpkin mixture. Add raisins. Gradually add flour. Knead the dough for about 4 minutes. Place in a bowl which has been sprayed with vegetable cooking spray and cover. Put in a warm place to rise to double its original size. Knead the bread lightly and place in sprayed loaf pan. Allow to rise again to double its size. Bake in a pre-heated 350° oven for 35 to 40 minutes. Test for doneness with a toothpick (if inserted toothpick comes out clean the bread is done). This bread has a hard, brown outside crust, with a bright mustard yellow inside.

16 Slices: 124 Calories per Slice; 1 gram Fat; 0 Cholesterol; 0 Saturated Fat.

Food Exchanges: 1-1/2 bread.

Quick Carrot Bread

1-3/4 cups flour
2 Tbs. brown sugar
1/3 tsp. brown sweetener
1/2 cup shredded carrot
1-1/2 tsp. baking powder
1-1/4 tsp. ground cinnamon
1/4 tsp. grated orange peel
1/4 tsp. salt
1/4 tsp. ground allspice
2 egg whites
1/4 cup skim milk
1/4 cup orange juice
2 Tbs. melted low-fat margarine
1 tsp. vanilla extract

In a medium-size bowl, combine flour, brown sugar, sweetener, carrot, baking powder, cinnamon, orange peel, salt, and allspice. In a separate bowl, thoroughly mix slightly beaten egg whites, milk, orange juice, margarine, and vanilla.

Quickly stir liquid ingredients into dry mixture, stirring only until dry ingredients are moistened. Turn into an 8x4″ loaf pan that has been sprayed with vegetable cooking spray. Bake in pre-heated 350° oven for 55 to 60 minutes. Cool for a few minutes and then remove from pan and cool completely on wire rack.

16 Slices: 68 Calories per Slice; 1 gram Fat; 0 Cholesterol; 0.2 grams Saturated Fat.

Food Exchanges: 1 bread.

Zucchini Bread

3/4 cup whole wheat flour
3/4 cup white flour
1/4 cup sugar
3 pkts. sweetener
1 tsp. baking powder
1/2 tsp. baking soda
1/4 tsp. salt
1 tsp. cinnamon
1/4 tsp. nutmeg
1/4 tsp. ground cloves
1 egg white
1/4 cup frozen egg substitute, thawed
1/4 cup vegetable oil
1-1/4 cups packed, finely-grated, unpeeled zucchini
1 tsp. vanilla
1/4 tsp. black walnut extract
1/3 cup raisins

In a large bowl, combine the whole wheat and white flours, sugar, baking powder, baking soda, salt, cinnamon, nutmeg, and cloves.

In another bowl, mix together the egg white, egg substitute, oil, zucchini, vanilla, and walnut extract. Add this mixture to the flour mixture, stirring the ingredients to combine them well. Stir in raisins. Pour the batter into a 9x5x3" loaf pan that has been sprayed with vegetable cooking spray. Bake the bread in pre-heated 350° oven for 50–60 minutes or until a toothpick inserted in the center of the bread comes out clean.

16 Slices: 99 Calories per Slice; 4 grams Fat; 0 Cholesterol; 0.6 grams Saturated Fat.

Food Exchanges: 1/2 bread; 1 fat.

Desserts

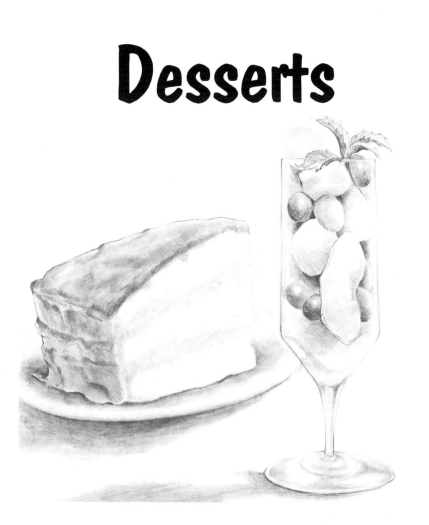

DESSERTS

You don't have to be terribly astute to notice that the largest section of this book is this one on desserts. For most of us who have a weight problem, desserts are our biggest pitfall. Well, I'm here to tell you that you can have your cake, or pie, or pudding, and eat it too, to contradict the old saying. We've taken literally thousands of calories out of these delicious desserts.

The most important thing in any weight maintenance or reduction program is to refrain from feeling sorry for yourself. If eating a dessert keeps you from feeling deprived, by all means have a dessert. Caution: Keep on hand only desserts that you eat with a spoon or a fork. Stay away from the stand-up finger-food types. I did not include cookie recipes in this book, although I found several that contained 45 to 90 calories per cookie. Do you know a single weight-problem person who can eat one cookie, or two? Most of you have eaten a batch of cookies in a day—one cookie at a time! Oops, they were all gone and the children weren't even home from school yet.

That is not quite as bad as the story a friend of mine told. While on one of her perennial diets, she baked her husband's favorite pie for his dinner. An hour or so before he was due home from work, my friend realized that she had eaten more than half of the pie, a small piece at a time while standing at the sink. She knew her husband would be terribly disappointed in her. What could she do? She did the only thing possible . . . she ate the rest of the pie to destroy the evidence. I plead guilty to a similar instance. I brought home several boxes of Dutch chocolate from Amsterdam for my husband. One night when I was roaming over the house during a sleepless night, I took one chocolate, then another, then another. I had to finish off the chocolates and throw away the package rather than have my husband find a half-empty box.

If you must have cookies in the house, get store-bought ones, those you don't like very much. Don't bake them yourself. You can eat a half dozen just taking them out of the cookie sheet—you know, the ones that have crumbled or are slightly misshapen. With all due respect to Erma Bombeck, broken cookies *do* contain calories!

I had planned to include a recipe for brownies. It seemed unAmerican not to. I pretty much followed a published low-calorie brownie recipe. It was pretty bad. It really wasn't worth the bother—nor the let-down which followed the mouth-watering anticipation.

Desserts are obviously the most difficult to take the calories out of and still have a tasty product. You don't even want to hear about the messes I made. When my husband, who is a dessert freak, didn't quite clean up his plate, I knew. It was back to the drawing board, or rather to the pastry board, for me.

Along the way I picked up a few tips which might be helpful to you. In most cooked desserts, it is recommended by the sugar substitute companies that you use a small amount of sugar and then extend it with a sugar substitute. The Sweet'n Low people told me that when you use Sweet'n Low in baking, you should decrease the dry ingredients by 20–25%, or increase the liquid by 20–25%. They suggested that you might want to add the equivalent of one extra egg or two egg whites, if they are part of your recipe.

I learned the hard way to measure sugar substitutes very carefully. When using sweetener in bulk, it is very easy to use too much, with bitter disastrous results. If the recipe calls for one teaspoon of sweetener, level it off with a knife.

It is also easy to err in the other direction and not use a sufficient amount. Remember that one teaspoon in a recipe is not interchangeable with one packet. It takes three packets to make one teaspoon of substitute sweetener in bulk.

In the dessert recipes where there is no prolonged nor intense heat involved, you may use your own preference of artificial sweeteners. If there is prolonged heat involved, however, it is necessary to ascertain if the sweetener is suitable for baking or prolonged heat. The label on the box will indicate the use for which the product is intended. Please read the labels for yourself.

Egg products are essential ingredients in many desserts. We have used egg substitutes freely. The term "egg substitute" is a misnomer inasmuch as all the egg substitutes I have worked with contain 99% real egg products, mostly egg whites. I guess we could simply use egg whites, but I like the yellow color and consistency of egg substitutes. There are several egg substitutes on the market, found not only in the frozen section, but unfrozen in the dairy section. The equivalency is: 1/4 cup egg substitute equals one whole egg. The calorie ratio: 25 calories in egg substitute to 70 calories in one whole egg. Not too significant, but the difference in cholesterol is zero to 240 mg. in one egg—almost the entire daily allowance of 300 mg. for cholesterol-restricted diets. My sister Norma, who simply couldn't throw away food, saved her egg yolks and made chess pies for her grandchildren. Betty White, as Rose, the inimitable dumb blond–grey panther in Golden Girls, saved her egg yolks to give to the homeless. You can imagine what Dorothy had to say about that. I go along with my sister Millie who, since suffering a serious heart attack, tosses her egg yolks down the drain. Just recently, however, I've experimented with mixing egg yolk with my watercolors with some interesting results. Never fear, Mr. Wyeth.

We will now address the subject of fats in baking. Right off, we have eliminated lard and all animal fats as well as butter, vegetable shortenings, margarines which contain cholesterol, palm oil, coconut oil, and all other oils which to the best of our knowledge contain substantial amounts of cholesterol, or which cause cholesterol buildup in the body. For the butter flavor, we are substituting Molly McButter, Butter Buds, or McCormick's Best 'O Butter.

Folks, that does not leave a lot to work with in baking.

In conjunction with cobblers, pies, and cheesecakes, I have given you a few pie-crust recipes, using graham crackers and low-fat margarine, or flour with a small amount of vegetable oil. The graham cracker crusts work well with cream pies or cheesecakes. The flour and oil pie crusts are adequate for fruit cobblers. You won't win a blue ribbon at the County Fair with these pie crusts. As we have said earlier, "life is a trade off." As for me, I will happily trade those light flaky pie crusts for a nicer body and a stronger heart.

FRUITS

Despite giving you 40 recipes for pies, puddings, cakes, and fluffs, I personally will take fresh fruit as the dessert of choice most of the time. Fresh fruit is easy to prepare; it looks good, tastes good, and is good for you.

Take a couple of extra minutes and serve fresh fruit in unusual and attractive presentations. Serve it on a dessert plate, or on a fruit platter suitable for a centerpiece.

Following are a few tips and comments about my favorite fresh fruits.

Apples. If there were only one fruit in the world, it would have to be apples. Never let it be said that I would try to rewrite the Bible, but I'll bet that Eve would have chosen the apple without the egging on from that wily old snake.

Apples are attractive; varied in appearance, taste, and texture; versatile both raw and cooked; and available all year round. The whole country went into collective shock a year or so ago when the Alar scare threatened the safety—and thus the sanctity—of the apple. Apple growers have stopped using Alar, the supposedly cancer-causing insecticide. Apples have now regained their place as the all-American fruit and the subject of the old refrain, "An apple a day keeps the doctor away."

Fresh Pineapple. Wash carefully but do not remove the green fronds. Cut lengthwise in eight or ten pieces, including the fronds. I use my electric knife for this purpose. Cut the pineapple fruit out of each piece. Cut into bite-size pieces and return to the shell. If you can afford the calories, sprinkle one teaspoon of red sugar granules over the pineapple. Arrange in a round serving tray, cartwheel fashion with leaves toward center. Place frozen green grapes or strawberries between slices.

Green Grapes. Break up a bunch of seedless grapes into small clusters of about ten each. Put into a freezer bag and freeze. Take out of freezer immediately before serving. The frosty grapes add a crisp coolness to a summer meal. Grapes are relatively high in calories, 35 to 40 for ten grapes, depending upon the variety.

Blueberries. Blueberries make a wonderful finger-food snack. Home frozen blueberries are even better. Wash the fruit and pat dry with a paper towel. Place in freezer bag. They are great for TV snacks. You can have a whole cupful of blueberries for 90 calories.

Bananas. Bananas are high in calories, about 100 for one banana. Bananas are my personal "red light" food. They are likely to set me off on an uncontrollable eating spree. My own solution to that is that I freeze them. In that way I cannot eat them so fast. Besides, they taste like a dessert when they are frozen. Freeze firm ripe bananas by simply sticking them in the freezer; take them out immediately before serving. Slice crosswise with a sharp knife. The brown peel will sluff off as the banana begins to thaw or it can be cut off with a knife. To make banana Popsicles, cut off one end and insert a Popsicle stick. Place in freezer bag and freeze. When ready to serve, dip the banana in warm water to loosen the peel.

Raspberries. It is difficult to find raspberries in my part of Texas, but last summer my favorite supermarket carried them for a few weeks. One whole cup—only 70 calories. One whole cup—$3.95, and worth every penny.

Cantaloupes. Cantaloupes are a dieter's delight. You can have one-half of a 5-1/2" cantaloupe for only 80 calories. Sometimes I slice them in the old-fashioned way and eat them with blackeyed peas, okra, and cornbread. Other times I cut them in halves and eat them with a serrated grapefruit spoon.

Grapefruit. The Texas Ruby Red grapefruit from the Rio Grande Valley are the best in the world. One year I received the bushel of grapefruit which I had ordered for Christmas, and for a couple of days I was being very generous handing out a couple or so to various friends and relatives. Then came the big freeze of December 1989. My generosity came to a screeching halt. I crammed the remaining grapefruit into my refrigerator and doled out one every other day to me and my husband, as I grieved over my personal loss as a consumer, as well as the loss to the growers and to the workers who harvest the Valley fruit and vegetables. Grapefruit are superb as a breakfast fruit, as a dessert for lunch, and as a salad for dinner. I could give you some suggestions about dripping a teaspoon of honey over the grapefruit, then broiling it, but that would only add calories. When I serve a grapefruit half, I simply cut it across the grain, cut around each segment, and furnish a serrated grapefruit spoon.

Let me give you a couple of tips about peeling and cutting grapefruit. First, an easy and quick way to peel segments for salads: With a sharp knife, or preferably a good serrated knife, peel the grapefruit, being sure the knife cuts just below the membrane of the segments; then cut out each segment lengthwise, leaving all the membrane intact. Grapefruit segments are a wonderful alternative in a green salad during the winter months, when tomatoes tend to be anemic and tasteless.

A great way to cut grapefruit so that it can be served as a finger food is to cut it lengthwise, then slice each half across the grain into four or five slices. You can then pick up each piece and eat it out of the peel.

Peaches. This was the fruit of my childhood—fresh peaches all summer from the time that the early peaches began to turn, and canned peaches all winter. You can have a medium peach for 40 calories and a cupful of slices for only 65 calories. Last summer I had a few extra peaches and no time to prepare them for freezing. I washed them, patted them dry, put them in a freezer bag, and placed them in my freezer. When ready to serve them, I dunk them in hot water for a second and the skin comes right off. They taste almost like fresh peaches.

Kiwi Fruit. That's an interesting little fruit—ugly and hairy on the outside and so beautiful on the inside, with the light yellow center that looks and tastes like a banana, ringed with shiny black seeds, and surrounded by emerald green pulp. No one but the master artist from above could have designed such a fruit. Kiwi fruit is used largely for garnish for desserts, fruit salads, or in fruit punch. This is one case when the garnish is more tasty than the garnished.

Pears. The once-lowly pear seems to be coming into its own. When I was a child, every farmhouse had a pear tree out back. The pears were hard and tasteless, not much good for eating, but in the spring the white blossoms exuded a sweet fragrance that wafted through our bedroom windows. In the summertime the pear tree provided wonderful shade for us when we played making mud pies or mumbly peg. My mother made pear preserves, because she made preserves out of almost everything. Nowadays, there are many kinds of pears on the market, and the newspaper and magazine food sections are full of exotic recipes for them, especially in the fall.

Strawberries. What a beautiful fruit! And you can have a whole cupful for only 55 calories. Sometimes they are just too pretty to chop up. I wash them carefully, leaving the stem and leaves on. They are eaten by holding onto the stem. Sometimes I slice them and eat them with a sweetener and low-fat milk.

There are many other fine fruits such as oranges, with 65 calories in a small orange; papayas, one cup of cubes for 55 calories; plums; nectarines; and of course the watermelon. In the summertime, I'll take my dessert calories in watermelon any time. You can have a 4x8″ wedge for 110 calories.

I have given you several recipes for cooked fruit desserts and salads. I hope you will try some of them, and that you will like them. Any way you slice it, when you cook the fruit, you will be gilding the lily.

—— Waldorf Astoria Chocolate Cake ——

Before I give you the recipe for this delicious cake, I must tell you a story as it was related to me, not once but several times by different people in different parts of the country. Each time, the person relating the tale swore it was a true story. It went like this:

"My friend's cousin made a recent trip to New York City and stayed at the Waldorf Astoria, where she ate this super delicious chocolate cake in the hotel restaurant. After she came home, she wrote a letter to the Waldorf Astoria, telling them what a good time she had had in New York, and thanking them for their hospitality. She wrote that she had enjoyed the meals in the dining room, especially that super delicious chocolate cake. Would they please send her the recipe. She would appreciate it a lot and she thanked them in advance for their neighborliness.

"Sure enough, in a couple of weeks she received a letter from the Waldorf Astoria with a copy of the recipe—and along with it there was a bill. Would you believe, it was a bill for $200 for the recipe? My friend's cousin gave my friend a copy, and my friend made a copy for me."

This was the story as related to me in the Rio Grande Valley of Texas. That was some time toward the end of the 1940's. Within two weeks, I heard the same story almost verbatim when we stopped in Dallas on our way to Illinois. Sure enough, while visiting relatives in Illinois, I heard it again. And that was before Xerox machines, Fax machines, and before I had ever seen a television set. Each person who told the story surreptitiously gave me a copy of the recipe, swearing me to secrecy lest the folks at the Waldorf Astoria charge all of us for fraudulent possession.

The story always ended with, "Would you believe that the cake is made with Miracle Whip?"

Recently I repeated this story to an affluent friend of mine in Upstate New York. She said she heard the same story during the nineteen forties, but the price was $2,000. Oh, well, we won't quibble over the price. The price for you is the cost of this book. And I'm sure that the folks at Kraft would just love for you to Fax it to all your friends and cousins.

A similar story surfaced a few years ago about a Neiman Marcus cookie. Sorry, folks, there was no way that I could take the calories out of that one.

I cannot tell a lie, it wasn't easy to take the calories out of the Waldorf Astoria cake, either. I tried several times with Kraft Lite and other low-calorie salad dressings and had a flop every time. Finally I decided to use real Miracle Whip and it worked . . . well, it's adequate, if you are hungry enough for chocolate cake. We might best call it "Motel 6 Chocolate Cake."

1 cup Kraft Miracle Whip Salad Dressing
1-3/4 cups flour
1/4 cup sugar
12 pkts. Sweet One
1 tsp. baking soda
3 tsp. baking powder
4 Tbs. cocoa
2 tsp. vanilla extract
1/4 tsp. salt
1 cup water

Place Miracle Whip, sugar, and Sweet One in a mixing bowl. Beat with an electric beater until well blended. In another bowl sift flour, baking soda, baking powder, salt, and cocoa together. Add one-third of the water to Miracle Whip mixture. Beat thoroughly, then add one-third of flour mixture and beat well. Continue to add water and flour alternately, beating after each addition. Add vanilla extract.

Spray two 9″ cake pans with vegetable cooking spray. Line pans with wax paper circles. Pour equal amount of batter into each pan and bake in pre-heated 325° oven for 20 minutes. Test for doneness by inserting a toothpick; it should come out fairly clean. Cool in pan for a few minutes. Run a table knife around the sides to loosen. Turn out on rack or cake plate. Be very careful as the layers are very fragile.

Icing

> 1 (1.3-oz.) pkg. chocolate Jello Instant Pudding
> (sugar-free)
> 7/8 cup cold skim milk

Pour 7/8 cup of cold milk into a small mixing bowl. Gradually add Chocolate Instant Pudding mix, beating with an electric beater. Remember that this is less than half the amount of milk called for to make pudding; therefore, the mixture will be stiffer than pudding. Ice the first layer of cake; add the second layer and ice it.

12 Servings: 163 Calories per Serving: 7 grams Fat; 6 mg. Cholesterol; 1 gram Saturated Fat.

Food Exchanges: 1 bread; 2 fat.

Apple Cobbler

5 cooking apples
1/8 cup sugar
1/2 tsp. Sweet'n Low
1/2 tsp. cinnamon
2 tsp. lemon juice
1/4 cup water

Peel, core, and slice apples. Place in 9″ baking dish. Combine sugar, sugar substitute, cinnamon, water, and lemon juice. Sprinkle over apple slices. Bake for 30 minutes at 350°.

Crust

1 cup flour
1 tsp. baking powder
2 Tbs. low-fat margarine
1/4 cup skim milk

Sift flour and baking powder. Cut in margarine. Slowly add milk, stirring constantly. Make dough into a ball. Place ball between two sheets of waxed paper, lightly dusted with flour. Roll out dough, and slice in 1″ wide strips. Place on top of cooked apples. Raise oven heat to 450° and bake for another 20 minutes.

8 Servings: 131 Calories per Serving; 2 grams Fat; 0 Cholesterol; 0.3 grams Saturated Fat.

Food Exchanges: 1 bread; 1 fruit.

Apple Crisp Ring

6 small baking apples (2 Granny, 2 medium red, 2
    dark red)
1/4 cup flour
1/4 cup oatmeal, uncooked
1 Tbs. wheat germ
3 Tbs. light brown sugar
1/2 tsp. Sweet'n Low, or 5 pkts.
1/2 tsp. cinnamon
1/8 tsp. nutmeg
3 Tbs. low-fat margarine
1 red apple for garnish (not counted in total
    calories)
1 oz. Monterey Jack cheese, low-fat, low-cal

Spray a 9" springform pan with vegetable cooking spray. In a small bowl, combine flour, oatmeal, wheat germ, brown sugar, Sweet'n Low, cinnamon, and nutmeg. With two knives, or a pastry blender (or with your hands, like I do), cut in margarine until mixture resembles coarse crumbs.

Slice applies in 1/2" slices, core but do not peel. Use medium red apples for first layer. Arrange apple slices in wagonwheel fashion with slight overlap around outer edge of pan, leaving the center empty. Repeat the process with slices of Granny apples or other green baking apples, placing them between the bottom row slices.

Sprinkle 2/3 of the flour-oatmeal crumbs over the slices. Use the dark red apples for the top row, arranging the slices peel-side up around the ring. Place the whole red apple for garnish in the center of the ring, after having made a few sharp cuts down its sides to prevent its bursting open while cooking. Add the remaining crumbs over the apple slices. Bake in a pre-heated 350° oven for 35 to 40 minutes.

While still warm, insert a knife around the edges of the pan. Take the outside of the springform pan off, and place bottom of pan, with the apple crisp intact, onto a pretty serving plate. This makes a beautiful presentation for an autumn dinner party. Be sure to bring to the table before cutting to serve.

Offer 1/6 oz. of low-fat, low-cal Monterey Jack cheese with each serving. For your family or guests who do not have to worry about calories or cholesterol, you can serve a scoop of ice cream . . . only if you have overcome a craving for ice cream yourself.

The center apple is for garnish only. The next day you can have it for lunch, and simply count it as a fruit.

6 Servings: 149 Calories per Serving: 4 grams Fat; 2 mg. Cholesterol; 1 gram Saturated Fat.

Food Exchanges: 1/2 bread; 1 fruit; 1 fat.

Apple Brown Betty

2 cups bread crumbs
3 Tbs. melted low-fat margarine
4 apples, medium
1 Tbs. lemon juice
1/2 tsp. lemon rind, grated
1/4 cup brown sugar
1 tsp. sugar substitute
1/3 cup hot water

Make crumbs from day-old bread by using the food processor or by simply crumbling it with your hands. Apple Brown Betty is an old-fashioned recipe, dating back to the early settlers, and they did not have food processors.

Combine crumbs and margarine in nonstick skillet over low heat. Continue over the heat, stirring constantly, until the crumbs are light brown. Place one-third of crumbs in 6x10" baking dish, sprayed with vegetable cooking spray.

Peel and slice apples. Arrange one-half of the apples over the bread crumbs. Sprinkle with half of the lemon juice, lemon rind, and sugar combination. Add second layer of one third of the crumbs and the remaining apples. Repeat the lemon and sugar layer. Sprinkle the remaining bread crumbs on top. Pour 1/3 cup of hot water over the entire mixture. Bake in pre-heated 375° oven for 30 to 40 minutes. Serve warm, with or without a whipped topping. (Topping calories not counted below.)

8 Servings: 174 Calories per Serving: 3.5 grams Fat; 0 Cholesterol; 0.7 grams Saturated Fat.

Food Exchanges: 1 bread; 1/2 fruit; 1/2 fat.

Apple Pandowdy

You have probably heard of Apple Pandowdy all your life, but I'll wager that few of you have eaten it, and fewer have cooked it. That will change after you have seen this recipe, which is easy to prepare and has less than half the calories of a regular apple pie.

When you taste it, you'll burst into song, just like Dinah Shore,

" . . . and apple pandowdy,
It makes your eyes light up,
And your tummy say howdy,
. . . and apple pandowdy,
I can't get enough of that wonderful stuff."

1/3 cup brown sugar
2 tsp. Sweet'n Low, brown
1/4 tsp. salt
2 Tbs. flour
1 Tbs. Butter Buds
1 tsp. vinegar
1 cup water
1/2 tsp. cinnamon
1/4 tsp. nutmeg
1 tsp. lemon juice
1 tsp. vanilla extract
5 cups apples, pared and sliced

Dough

1 cup flour
2 tsp. baking powder
1/4 tsp. salt
2 Tbs. vegetable oil
4 tsp. Butter Buds, with 3 Tbs. water
1/3 cup skim milk

Make a sauce by mixing sugar, sweetener, 2 Tbs. of flour, and salt in a saucepan. Add vinegar and water, and Butter Buds with one cup water. Cook over low heat until thickened, stirring constantly. Add cinnamon, nutmeg, lemon juice, and vanilla. Set aside.

Mix 1 cup of flour, baking powder, and salt. Add oil, using pastry blender. When mixture has texture of crumbs, add milk. Stir just long enough to moisten.

Place apples in 12x8″ baking dish sprayed with vegetable-cooking spray. Pour sauce over apples. Drop dough by heaping teaspoons over all the apples. Bake in pre-heated 375° oven for 35 to 40 minutes until dough topping is brown. Serve warm. Top with Dessert Topping, if desired—like the one for Pumpkin Vanilla Pudding.

8 Servings: 183 Calories per Serving; 4 grams Fat; 0 Cholesterol; 0.5 grams Saturated Fat.

Food Exchanges: 1 bread; 1 fruit; 1 fat.

—Applesauce Oatmeal Coffee Cake—

This coffee cake went over great at the Monday Morning Circle meeting at the Presbyterian Church. I had bought doughnuts on my way to the meeting, just in case. The coffee cake was polished off, and not a doughnut was touched.

1-1/2 cups oatmeal, uncooked
1-1/4 cups flour
3/4 tsp. cinnamon

2 tsp. baking powder
3/4 tsp. baking soda
1 cup applesauce, unsweetened
1/2 cup skim milk
6 pkts. Sweet'n Low
2 Tbs. vegetable oil
1/4 cup egg substitute
1 egg white
1 Tbs. brown sugar
1/4 tsp. salt

Topping

1/4 cup oatmeal, quick, uncooked
1 Tbs. brown sugar
1/4 tsp. cinnamon
1 Tbs. low-fat margarine

Sift together flour, cinnamon, baking powder, baking soda, and salt. Add oats. Beat egg substitute, egg white, sugar, and sweetener together in a mixing bowl. Add oil and milk. Add flour and oats mixture. Stir only until ingredients are moistened. Pour into a 9x13" baking tin which has been sprayed with vegetable cooking spray.

Combine topping ingredients and sprinkle on top. Bake in preheated 350° oven for 25 minutes. Serve warm.

12 Servings: 138 Calories per Serving; 4 grams Fat; 0 Cholesterol; 0.5 grams Saturated Fat.

Food Exchanges: 1 bread; 1 fat.

Apricot Fluff

Apricot Fluff is my special gift to you. It is light and fluffy, pleasing to the eye and to the palate, and—best of all—it is low in calories and cholesterol. I tried, I really tried, to give you a recipe for apricot fried pies, which became my trademark

in *Mrs. Blackwell's Cookbook*. Each attempt was more disastrous than the last. Let's face it: You can't make fried pies
without using all that ol' grease. Besides that, they are a lot
of trouble to make and you probably haven't had any since
you were a child anyway. No point in starting now. Enjoy the
Apricot Fluff. It is easy to make and easy on your figure.

> *6 oz. dried apricots*
> *1 pkg. (0.3 oz.) orange Jello, sugar-free*
> *1 Tbs. sugar*
> *4 pkts. Sweet'n Low*
> *1/2 cup plain yogurt*
> *1/2 cup imitation sour cream*
> *2 egg whites*
> *4 drops almond extract*
> *1 kiwi for garnish*

Stew dried apricots in about 1-3/4 cups of water until tender,
about 25 minutes. Add sweetener. Puree apricots in their liquid in
blender or processor.

Prepare Jello by adding one cup of hot water and stir well.
When slightly cooled, add to apricot puree in blender and blend
well. Add yogurt and imitation sour cream. Add almond extract.
Pour into a bowl and place in refrigerator until partially congealed.

Beat egg whites with electric beater until soft peaks form. Add
sugar, one tablespoon at a time. Fold egg whites into Jello mixture.
Garnish with thin slices of kiwi.

*8 Servings: 110 Calories per Serving; 3 grams Fat; 0 Cholesterol;
2 grams Saturated Fat.*

Food Exchanges: 1 fruit; 1 fat.

Baked Apples

2 medium-size cooking apples
2 pkts. Sweet'n Low
1/2 tsp. Molly McButter
1/2 tsp. cinnamon
2 tsp. raisins
1/2 cup water or diet cherry soda

Scoop out the apple cores. Mix cinnamon with sweetener and sprinkle into the apple cores. Sprinkle in Molly McButter. Place apples upright in small baking dish, and pour 1/2 cup of water or diet soda over them. Bake at 350° for 20 to 25 minutes in conventional oven. For microwave baking, cover loosely and microwave on high for 2-1/2 to 3 minutes.

2 Servings: 96 Calories per Serving; 1 gram Fat; 0 Cholesterol; 0 Saturated Fat.

Food Exchanges: 1-1/2 fruit.

Berry Cobbler

I'm a berry picker from way back. Nothing gives me more pleasure than donning a straw hat and a long-sleeved shirt with a bucket over my arm and being alone among the berry vines on a country roadside. I can temporarily forget my deathly fear of snakes, my aching back, the inevitable chigger bites, my new manicure, and the problems in Central America or the Middle East in my quest for the perfect berry. If there are any berries left in my bucket by the time I get home, I'll make a berry cobbler.

This recipe is especially suitable for blueberries, blackberries, or cherries.

> 1 Tbs. cornstarch
> 1 cup water
> 1 tsp. sweetener
> 2 tsp. lemon juice
> 2 cups washed, fresh berries, or unsweetened
>   frozen berries partially thawed.
> 3/4 cup flour
> 1-1/2 tsp. baking powder
> 1/4 tsp. salt
> 2 Tbs. vegetable oil
> 6 Tbs. cold skim milk
> 2 Tbs. sugar

Combine cornstarch and water. Cook until thickened and clear. Add 1 tsp. sweetener, lemon juice, and berries. Mix well. Pour into an 8x8″ baking pan.

Sift together flour, 2 Tbs. sugar, baking powder, and salt. Add oil, and mix with a pastry blender until mixture resembles fine crumbs. Add cold milk and mix with a fork until combined, but do not over mix. Drop dough by spoonfuls onto the berries. Bake in pre-heated 425° oven for about 30 minutes or until biscuits are brown. Serve warm.

6 Servings: For blueberries and cherries: 151 Calories per Serving; 5 grams Fat; 0 Cholesterol.

For blackberries: 148 Calories per Serving; 5 grams Fat; 0 Cholesterol; 0.6 grams Saturated Fat.

Food Exchanges: 1 bread; 1/2 fruit; 1 fat.

Brandied Pumpkin Custard

1 can (12 oz.) evaporated skim milk
2 egg whites
1/4 cup frozen egg substitute, thawed
1/4 cup honey
2 Tbs. sugar
1/2 tsp. sweetener
1 tsp. vanilla
1 cup canned pumpkin
1/2 tsp. cinnamon
1/2 tsp. nutmeg
1/2 tsp. allspice
1/2 tsp. ground cloves
1/8 tsp. salt
1 tsp. brandy extract
Hot water

In a saucepan, heat milk until almost boiling. In a bowl, beat egg substitute and egg whites. Add honey, pumpkin, spices, sugar, sweetener, salt, and flavoring and blend well. Pour 1/2 cup of hot milk in the egg–pumpkin mixture. Mix well. Pour the egg mixture into the saucepan with the remainder of the milk. Stir until well blended.

Pour custard into individual custard cups which have been sprayed with vegetable cooking spray. Place custard cups in a pan with 3/4 of an inch of hot water and bake for about one hour, or until cake tester or knife inserted into center of cup comes out clean. May be served hot or cold.

Run a knife around side of custard cup to loosen, and invert onto a dessert plate.

6 Servings: 149 Calories per Serving; 1 gram Fat; 3 mg. Cholesterol; 0.4 grams Saturated Fat.
Food Exchanges: 1/2 meat; 1 bread; 1/2 milk.

Baked Custard

2 cups evaporated skim milk
1/4 cup frozen egg substitute
2 Tbs. sugar
4 pkts. Sweet'n Low
1/8 tsp. salt
1 tsp. vanilla extract
1/2 tsp. nutmeg
1/2 tsp. lemon extract
1 egg white

Scald skim milk. Beat egg substitute, egg white, sugar, sweetener, and salt until well blended. Add scalded milk, vanilla and lemon extracts. Pour into 5 custard cups which have been sprayed with vegetable cooking spray. Place cups in a pan of hot (not boiling) water, one inch deep. Sprinkle nutmeg over custard. Bake in pre-heated 325° oven until custard is set—about one hour. Test for doneness by gently pressing on top with finger.

5 Servings: 70 Calories per Serving; 2 grams Fat; 2 mg. Cholesterol; 0.4 grams Saturated Fat.

Food Exchanges: 1/2 fat; 1/2 milk.

Banana Pudding

My sister Millie took this banana pudding to the church supper, and the twenty-nine-year-old preacher, who had never had a reason to think about cholesterol or calories, just raved about the banana pudding. He insisted that his wife get the recipe, oblivious to the fact that the original old-fashioned country-cooking recipe had been changed into a diet dish.

One (12-oz.) can evaporated skim milk
1/2 cup fresh skim milk
2 egg whites
1/4 cup egg substitute
1/2 cup sugar
12 pkts. Sweet One
1/4 cup cornstarch
1 tsp. vanilla extract
10 graham crackers (double)
3 ripe bananas

Using an electric beater or hand beater, mix egg whites and egg substitute with sugar and sugar substitute. Mix the cornstarch with a small portion of the canned evaporated skim milk until smooth. Then add the rest of the canned milk and the regular skim milk. Blend the milk mixture with the egg and sugar mixture. Cook in saucepan over medium heat until mixture thickens. Add vanilla extract.

Line a 9x12" glass baking dish with five of the graham crackers. Add a layer of sliced bananas (about 1-1/2 bananas). Pour half of the pudding mixture over the bananas, repeat a second layer. Make this up a few hours before serving and cool in the refrigerator.

8 Servings: 219 Calories per Serving; 2 grams Fat; 2 mg. Cholesterol; 0.5 grams Saturated Fat.

Food Exchanges: 1 meat; 1 bread; 1/2 fruit; 1/2 milk.

Bread Pudding

4 slices of day-old white bread
1/2 cup egg substitute
1-1/2 cups skim milk, scalded
2 Tbs. sugar
1/2 tsp. Sweet'n Low
1/2 tsp. cinnamon
1/8 tsp. salt
1 egg white
1/2 tsp. lemon extract

Cut or tear bread in one-inch pieces. Place in baking dish sprayed with nonstick cooking spray. Place milk in a saucepan and heat until just before boiling point.

In a mixing bowl, beat egg substitute, sugar, sweetener, salt, lemon extract, and cinnamon. Gradually add the scalded milk, stirring as you do so.

Beat egg white until stiff. Gently fold into milk and egg mixture. Pour into the baking dish with the bread cubes. Bake in preheated 325° oven for about 45 minutes. Check at 40 minutes. Test by inserting a knife. If it comes out clean the pudding is done.

6 Servings: 113 Calories; 3 grams Fat; 1 mg. Cholesterol;
0.6 grams Saturated Fat.

Food Exchanges: 1/2 meat; 1/2 bread; 1/2 milk.

Lemon Sauce

2 Tbs. Jello vanilla pudding, instant sugar-free
1/2 cup water
1 tsp. Sugar-Free Crystal Light lemonade mix

Mix ingredients in a small bowl until well blended. Serve over warm bread pudding.

6 Servings: 9 Calories per serving.

Food Exchanges: Free.

Chocolate Fluff

1 envelope unflavored gelatin
1/4 cup cold water
1/4 tsp. salt
2 Tbs. sugar
3 Tbs. cocoa
1/4 cup egg substitute
2 egg whites
1 tsp. vanilla extract
1/2 tsp. sweetener
1/4 cup nonfat dry milk
1/4 cup cold water

Soften gelatin in cold water 5 minutes. Mix cocoa and sugar; add salt. Slowly add milk to cocoa mixture, stirring constantly to blend. Heat cocoa and milk over low heat until cocoa is completely mixed; heat to boiling point. Slowly pour heated mixture over egg substitute, stirring constantly to prevent lumping. Return mixture to saucepan and cook on low heat for one minute. Remove from heat and add gelatin, vanilla, and sweetener. Cool until slightly set.

Beat egg whites until stiff. In another small mixing bowl, combine powdered milk with 1/4 cup of cold water. Beat until consistency of whipped cream.

Fold beaten egg whites into cocoa–milk mixture. Then fold whipped powdered milk into mixture. Be sure that all is blended, but do not beat. Pour into sherbet dishes and chill thoroughly before serving.

6 Servings: 71 Calories per Serving; 2 grams Fat; 1 mg. Cholesterol; 0.5 grams Saturated Fat.

Food Exchanges: 1/2 meat; 1/2 milk.

Chocolate Sauce

Serve this sauce on puddings or ice cream. Makes 1-1/2 cups of sauce. This can also be used to make a chocolate milk shake.

3 Tbs. cocoa
1 Tbs. flour
1/8 tsp. salt
1-1/2 cups skim milk
1/2 tsp. sweetener
1 Tbs. sugar
1 tsp. Butter Buds
1 tsp. vanilla extract

Combine cocoa, flour, and salt in a saucepan. Add milk slowly, stirring until mixture is blended. Cook over low heat or in a double boiler, stirring constantly until mixture is thick and smooth. Remove from heat, and stir in sweetener, Butter Buds, and vanilla. Blend mixture thoroughly. Chill.

12 Servings: 2 Tbs. per Serving; 22 Calories per Serving; 0 Fat; 1 mg. Cholesterol; 0.2 grams Saturated Fat.

Food Exchanges: 1/4 milk.

Crustless German Cheesecake

2 Tbs. wheat germ
1-1/2 lbs. low-fat cottage cheese
1/2 cup egg substitute
1/3 cup cornstarch
2 tsp. vanilla
1/2 tsp. cinnamon
2 Tbs. honey
1/3 cup sugar
1 tsp. Sweet'n Low
2 Tbs. lemon juice
Grated peel of 1 lemon
3 egg whites

Spray springform pan with vegetable cooking spray. Mix wheat germ and cinnamon; sprinkle on bottom of pan.

In food blender or food processor, blend cottage cheese until smooth. Add egg substitute, honey, sweetener, sugar, cornstarch, lemon juice, vanilla, and lemon peel. Mix well. Pour into large bowl.

In another bowl, beat egg whites until stiff peaks form. Very gently fold the egg whites into the cottage cheese mixture. Do not over beat or you will deflate the whites.

Pour into springform pan. Bake in pre-heated 250° oven for 75 minutes or until center shows firmness when lightly touched. Turn off oven. Leave door closed and allow cake to stand for 30 minutes. Remove and cool. Chill before serving.

You may place 2 teaspoons of fruit spread, sweetened with fruit juice (substitute for preserves), on top for garnish and an extra touch of sweets. If you do, add the calories, about 16 per teaspoon, to your total.

16 Servings: 69 Calories per Serving; 1 gram Fat; 2 mg. Cholesterol; 0.4 grams Saturated Fat.

Food Exchanges: 1 meat; 1/2 bread.

Easy Applesauce Cake

2 cups unsweetened applesauce
9 double graham crackers
1 tsp. brown Sweet'n Low
3 Tbs. brown sugar
1 tsp. cinnamon
1/4 tsp. ginger
1/4 tsp. cloves

In a 9x9" casserole dish or baking pan, place 9 single graham crackers. Spoon 1/2 of the applesauce over the graham crackers. Sprinkle 2 tsp. of brown Sweet'n Low over the applesauce. Sprinkle 1/2 of the cinnamon, ginger, and cloves over the applesauce. Repeat a second layer of graham crackers, applesauce, sugar substitute, and spices. Cover and put into the refrigerator and let set for several hours. At serving time, top with Mock Whipped Cream Topping.

Mock Whipped Cream Topping

1 cup canned nonfat evaporated skim milk
1/2 tsp. vanilla
4 pkts. Sweet'n Low

Make the topping by pouring a cup of canned evaporated skim milk into a small mixing bowl. Place in the freezing section of the refrigerator until ice crystals begin to form. Take out and beat with electric mixer at high speed until peaks begin to form. Add sugar substitute and vanilla extract, and serve immediately.

9 Servings: 119 Calories per Serving; 1.3 grams Fat; 1.3 mg. Cholesterol; 0.4 grams Saturated Fat.

Food Exchanges: 3/4 bread; 1/2 fruit; 1/2 milk.

Glazed Fruit Dessert

This is a luscious, quick, and attractive dessert. You could use this quick recipe with all sorts of fresh and canned fruits. Be sure the canned fruits have no sugar added.

> 1 can chunk pineapple (16 oz.), unsweetened
> 1 can mandarin oranges (8 oz.)
> 2 bananas
> 1 cup fresh or frozen strawberries, sliced
> 1 pkg. instant lemon or vanilla pudding mix,
>   sugar-free

Drain pineapple and oranges, and reserve the liquids. Add bananas and strawberries to other fruit. Add liquids from the canned fruit to the pudding mix and stir until well blended. Fold blended pudding into the fruit until all fruit is coated. Chill.

You may add extra zest to this dessert by adding 1/4 tsp. low-calorie Tang powder to the vanilla pudding mix, before mixing.

6 Servings: 97 Calories per Serving; 0 Fats; 0 Cholesterol; 0 Saturated Fat.

Food Exchanges: 1/2 fruit.

Icebox Pumpkin Parfait

1 can (16 oz.) pumpkin
1 box instant vanilla pudding mix, sugar-free
1 cup Cool Whip, Lite
1 cup cold skim milk
1 tsp. pumpkin pie spice

Mix first five ingredients together with a hand beater, or an electric beater at low speed. Pour into custard cups or parfait glasses and refrigerate.

Topping

1/2 cup canned evaporated skim milk
1 pkt. sweetener
1/2 tsp. vanilla

Make topping by chilling canned skim milk until ice crystals form. Beat at high speed with electric beater. Add sweetener and vanilla. Prepare this immediately before serving or the lovely creamy topping will revert back to unappetizing canned milk.
Swirl topping onto the pumpkin parfait.

8 Servings: 64 Calories per Serving; 2 grams Fat; 1 mg. Cholesterol; 1 gram Saturated Fat.

Food Exchanges: 1/2 bread; 1/2 fat.

Luscious Cheesecake

Crust

4 double graham crackers
2 Tbs. melted low-fat margarine
1/2 tsp. cinnamon
1 pkt. sweetener

Crush graham crackers by putting them in a plastic bag and rolling with a rolling pin. Place in a small bowl and mix with melted margarine. (I do this best with my fingers.) Spray a springform pan with vegetable cooking spray. Place crumb crust on the bottom and tamp down with your fingers or the back of a spoon. Bake in 300° oven for four or five minutes. Set aside.

Filling

4 cups cottage cheese, low-fat
2 envelopes (2 Tbs.) unflavored gelatin
2 Tbs. sugar
2 tsp. sweetener
1/2 cup egg substitute
1 cup skim milk
1 tsp. vanilla extract
1 tsp. lemon extract
1 tsp. grated orange rind
2 egg whites
1/8 tsp. salt

Place cottage cheese in blender or food processor, with 1/2 cup of milk. Blend until smooth. Pour into a large mixing bowl. Sprinkle the gelatin over the other half cup of milk in a saucepan. Heat the milk and gelatin over medium heat until gelatin is dissolved. Mix sugar and sweetener with egg substitute, and gradually add to milk and gelatin mixture, stirring constantly. Continue to cook for about five minutes. Add salt, vanilla, and lemon extract.

Add the gelatin mixture to the cottage cheese, and blend with an electric mixer on low speed. Whip egg whites until stiff; gently fold into cottage cheese mixture.

Pour the mixture into the springform pan, and place, lightly covered, in the refrigerator. Refrigerate for at least five hours, until completely set.

Cherry Topping

> 1 cup sour cherries, water-packed
> 1 cup cherry liquid
> 1 Tbs. sugar
> 1 tsp. sweetener
> 1 Tbs. cornstarch
> 1/2 tsp. almond flavoring
> Red food coloring

Place liquid, sugar, sweetener, and cornstarch in saucepan and cook on medium heat until it begins to thicken slightly. Add cherries, almond flavoring, and a few drops of red food coloring. Continue cooking until cherries are heated through. The red food coloring is optional—however, without it the cherries will be a washed-out reddish brown. When the cheesecake is completely set, add the topping. Calorie content with Cherry Topping:

12 Servings: 135 Calories per Serving; 3 grams Fat; 4 mg. Cholesterol; 1 gram Saturated Fat.

Food Exchanges: 1 meat; 1 bread.

Pineapple Topping

> 2 cups crushed pineapple, no sugar added
> 4 Tbs. vanilla Jello Pudding Mix, sugar-free

Drain the pineapple juice into a bowl and mix with vanilla pudding. When blended, add pineapple.

When the cheesecake is completely set, add the topping. Calorie count with Pineapple Topping:

> 12 Servings: 136 Calories per Serving; 3 grams Fat; 4 mg. Cholesterol; 1 gram Saturated Fat.

> Food Exchanges: 1 meat; 1 bread.

——————— Mock Indian Pudding ———————

You're going to love this new version of a very old-fashioned recipe. The ingredients, although basically the same, would not be recognized by the early Americans who introduced this pudding. They used Indian meal (cornmeal), whole milk, eggs, butter, spices, and sugar instead of corn-flakes, skim milk, egg beaters, sugar substitute, and margarine. Only the spices were the same, but the settlers had to grind them first. If they had wanted to use a flavoring, it would have been rose water.

Spices were used in abundance by those who could afford them, and they served several purposes during the post-Revolutionary days: Spices provided a rich taste to the food, they reduced the saltiness of meat preserved with salt, and they added a bit of zest to otherwise tasteless dried food. Another important function of spices was to disguise the taste and odor of near-rancid food in pre-refrigeration days.

1/4 cup egg substitute
1/2 cup light molasses
2 Tbs. brown sugar
1 tsp. Sweet'n Low
1/2 tsp. ground cinnamon
1/4 tsp. ground cloves
1/4 tsp. ginger
1/4 tsp. salt
1 tsp. vanilla
3 cups skim milk
4 cups cornflakes, coarsely crushed
Water

Combine egg substitute, molasses, sugar, sweetener, salt, cloves, cinnamon, and ginger. Add skim milk and blend well. I like to use an electric beater for this.

Crush the cornflakes ever so slightly and add to mixture. Pour into an 8x8" baking dish sprayed with vegetable cooking spray. Place pan in 9x13" metal baking pan filled with 3/4 inch of water. Bake in pre-heated 350° oven for one hour. Serve warm, with or without skim milk topping.

8 Servings: 154 Calories per Serving; 1 gram Fat; 2 mg. Cholesterol; 0.2 grams Saturated Fat.

Food Exchanges: 1 bread; 1/2 milk.

Oatmeal Banana Cake

2 cups oatmeal
1/4 cup flour
1/2 cup sugar
1 tsp. Sweet'n Low
2-1/2 tsp. baking powder
1/2 tsp. baking soda
1/2 tsp. salt
3 Tbs. vegetable oil
1 pkt. Butter Buds (1/2 oz.) plus 1/4 cup water
1/4 cup frozen egg substitute
4 or 5 ripe bananas
1 tsp. vanilla

Mash bananas in a bowl. Sift flour, sugar, sweetener, baking powder, soda, and salt. Add oatmeal. In another bowl, mix oil, egg substitute, and Butter Buds. Add one half of the bananas to the egg substitute and beat with electric beater on medium speed for about three minutes.

Add flour–oatmeal mixture, and continue beating for a couple of minutes. Add the additional bananas and vanilla and beat another three minutes. Pour batter into a tube pan or springform pan sprayed with vegetable cooking spray, and bake in preheated 350° oven for 45 minutes. Test after 40 minutes by inserting knife in cake; if it comes out clean, the cake is done.

Cool cake on rack for ten minutes. Loosen around the edges with a knife and turn out on rack to cool.

16 Servings: 126 Calories per Serving; 4 grams Fat; 0 Cholesterol; 0.6 grams Saturated Fat.

Food Exchanges: 1/2 bread; 1 fat.

Oat Crunch Topping

May be used as a topping for fruit or puddings, or for a cheesecake.

1-1/2 cups regular oats
1/2 cup unprocessed bran
1/2 cup wheat germ
1 Tbs. ground cinnamon
1 Tbs. low-fat margarine
1 Tbs. honey
2 pkts. sweetener

Melt margarine and mix with honey. Add other ingredients and mix well. Spread out on a baking sheet and bake in pre-heated 350° oven for about 10 minutes.

Makes 2-1/2 cups; at 1 Tbs. per Serving: 21 Calories; 0 Fat; 0 Cholesterol; 0 Saturated Fat.

Food Exchanges: 1/2 fat.

Orange Delight

1 cup crushed pineapple, unsweetened, drained
1 cup cottage cheese, low-fat, small curd
1 (0.3 oz.) pkg. sugar-free orange-flavored gelatin
1 cup canned evaporated skim milk
1 kiwi fruit

Put canned milk in small deep bowl and place in the freezer. When milk has formed ice crystals, beat with an electric beater until the consistency of whipped cream.

Sprinkle gelatin over the cottage cheese, and gently fold all into whipped milk. Refrigerate for 3 or 4 hours until congealed. Place in individual dessert bowls and garnish with slices of kiwi fruit.

4 Servings: 133 Calories per Serving; 1 gram Fat; 7 mg. Cholesterol; 1 gram Saturated Fat.

Food Exchanges: 1 meat; 1/2 fruit; 1/2 milk.

——————— Peach Cobbler ———————

Crust

1-1/2 cups flour
1/4 tsp. salt
2 Tbs. plus 1 tsp. vegetable oil
1 tsp. Molly McButter
1 Tbs. ice water

In a mixing bowl, combine flour, salt, and Molly McButter. Cut in oil, using a pastry blender or two knives, until the mixture is the size of small peas. Add ice water gradually, mixing dough with a fork. Roll out dough on a lightly floured dough board. Cut strips about 1-1/4 inch wide to place on top of the fruit.

Filling

2 qts. sliced peaches, fresh or frozen
2/3 cup water
1/4 cup sugar
4 pkts. sweetener
1/2 tsp. cinnamon
2 tsp. flour

Place peaches and water in a saucepan. Cook until peaches are heated through. Mix sugar, sweetener, cinnamon, and flour in a separate bowl. Place heated peaches in a 7x11" casserole baking dish. Sprinkle sugar and flour mixture over the peaches, then lay the strips of crust on top. Bake in pre-heated 350° oven for 30 to 40 minutes, or until crust is a light golden brown.

8 Servings: 221 Calories per Serving; 4 grams Fat; 0 Cholesterol; 1 gram Saturated Fat.

Food Exchanges: 1 bread; 1-1/2 fruit; 1 fat.

—————————— Piña Colada Pie ——————————

1 (8 oz.) can crushed pineapple, unsweetened
2 Tbs. sugar
3 pkts. Sweet'n Low
4 oz. low-fat cottage cheese
4 oz. low-fat plain yogurt
1/2 cup skim milk
1 tsp. rum flavoring
1/4 tsp. coconut extract
1 (3-1/2 oz.) sugar-free instant vanilla pudding
*   mix.*

Drain pineapple, reserving juice. In an electric blender, blend cottage cheese and yogurt until creamy. In a mixing bowl, beat yogurt and cottage cheese mixture with sugar and Sweet'n Low until smooth. Add milk, reserved pineapple juice, rum and coconut extracts. Blend well. Add pudding mix, beating one to two minutes longer. Stir in pineapple. Pour filling into baked graham cracker crust. Chill four hours.

Graham Cracker Crust

    6 double graham crackers
    2 Tbs. low-fat margarine

Crush graham crackers with a rolling pin. Mix with margarine. Place in bottom of 8" pie pan and pat on bottom and sides with the back of a spoon. Bake in 350° oven for about five minutes. Be very careful that crust does not burn.

Serves 8.
Without crust: 46 Calories per Serving; 0 Fat; 2 mg. Cholesterol.

Food Exchanges: 1/2 milk.

With Graham Cracker Crust: 83 Calories per Serving; 2 grams Fat; 2 mg. Cholesterol; 1 gram Saturated Fat.

Food Exchanges: 1 bread.

—— Pineapple Upside-Down Cake ——

I served this cake to my mixed bridge group. It received rave reviews, both before and after I told them it was going into my low-calorie cookbook. I was so happy to find a pineapple upside-down cake which I can include.

Pineapple upside-down cake—then chock full of calories and cholesterol—was very popular during the Fifties, and was a special favorite of my young children.

Topping

    2 Tbs. light brown sugar
    2 Tbs. low-fat margarine
    1 can (8 oz.) sliced pineapple, no sugar added, drained

Cake

> 2/3 cup sifted flour
> 1-1/2 tsp. baking powder
> 1/4 tsp. salt
> 2 Tbs. vegetable cooking oil
> 1 tsp. dry Butter Buds
> 1/3 cup skim milk
> 1/8 cup egg substitute
> 1 tsp. vanilla extract
> 1/4 cup sugar
> 1 tsp. Sweet'n Low
> 2 egg whites

Spray a 9″ round cake pan with vegetable cooking spray. (I use a springform pan.) In a small bowl, stir together brown sugar and 2 Tbs. margarine. Spread in bottom of cake pan. With paper towel, pat pineapple slices dry. Arrange in bottom of pan.

Mix flour, baking powder, and salt in a small bowl. Set aside. In a large bowl, beat egg substitute, skim milk, oil, Sweet'n Low, and vanilla with electric mixer. Gradually add flour mixture with milk–substitute egg mixture. Beat on medium speed until smooth.

In another small bowl, beat egg whites until soft peaks form. Gradually add sugar and continue beating until stiff. Fold beaten egg whites into batter using low speed.

Bake in pre-heated 350° oven for 20 to 25 minutes or until toothpick inserted in cake comes out clean. Cool for about five minutes before turning upside-down onto a cake plate. Remove cake pan carefully to be sure that pineapple remains in place.

8 Servings: 113 Calories per Serving; 5 grams Fat; 0 Cholesterol; 1 gram Saturated Fat.

Food Exchanges: 1/2 bread; 1/2 fruit; 1 fat.

Persimmon Pudding

Persimmon pudding was a favorite fall dessert of my first husband's Illinois relatives. They would not recognize this persimmon pudding. First of all, they used wild persimmons which were about the size of an English walnut and were inedible until after the first frost. Before the frost, they had a slightly bitter taste and made your mouth draw up. In the second place, our relatives used lots of sugar in their persimmon puddings.

My sister Jennie gave me some big beautiful persimmons off her tree. She gave me a hint which I will pass on to you: You can put them in the freezer until time to use them . . . that sorta' takes the place of the first frost.

1 cup persimmon pulp
1/4 cup egg substitute
1 Tbs. melted margarine
1 cup skim milk
1/4 cup sugar
3/4 cup flour
1/2 tsp. baking soda
1-1/2 tsp. Sweet'n Low
1/2 tsp. salt
1/2 tsp. nutmeg
1/2 tsp. cinnamon

Peel persimmons and take out the seeds and any hard core. Mash them or blend in blender with about one half cup of the milk. Place in a bowl and add the remaining milk and margarine.

Mix and sift together flour, soda, sugar, sweetener, salt, and spices. Combine with liquid mixture, beating with electric mixer until well blended. Pour into an 8x8" baking pan sprayed with vegetable cooking spray. Bake in pre-heated 350° oven for about 45 minutes. Test for doneness by lightly pressing finger on top. You may serve warm or cold, with or without Topping. (See Ice Box Pumpkin Parfait Topping. Topping is not included in calorie count.)

8 Servings: 132 Calories per serving; 2 grams Fat; 1 mg. Cholesterol; 0.5 grams Saturated Fat.

Food Exchanges: 1 bread; 1/2 fruit; 1 fat.

—— Pineapple–Strawberry Dessert ——

2 (0.3 oz.) pkgs. sugar-free strawberry Jello
3 cups boiling water
1 cup whole frozen strawberries, partially thawed
4 pkts. Sweet'n Low
1-1/2 cups canned crushed pineapple, no sugar added
One medium banana, mashed
1 cup plain yogurt, low-fat, vanilla or unflavored

Dissolve Jello in boiling water. In blender, grind strawberries. Add strawberries, pineapple, mashed banana, and sweetener to gelatin mixture. Mix well. Pour the gelatin mixture into a 9x9" square pan or a comparable size oblong pan. Place in the refrigerator until firm. Stir the yogurt; then spread on top of the gelatin. Place back in the refrigerator until time to serve.

6 Servings: 70 Calories per Serving; 0 Fat; 0 Cholesterol; 0 Saturated Fat.

Food Exchanges: 1 fruit; 1/3 milk.

Prune Whip

2 cups cooked prunes, pitted (you may substitute apricots)
1 tsp. grated lemon rind
2 tsp. lemon juice
4 Tbs. confectioners' sugar
2 pkts. Sweet'n Low
4 stiff-beaten egg whites

Cook prunes by putting in a saucepan, covering with water, and letting soak overnight. Turn on heat and let come to a boiling point. Turn off heat and leave prunes on burner until cool. Mash prunes to a pulp. Add lemon juice and rind and 2 Tbs. of sugar and the Sweet'n Low. Blend well. Beat egg whites until stiff. Gradually add remaining sugar to egg whites. Pile lightly into baking dish sprayed with vegetable cooking spray. Bake in 350° oven for 20 to 30 minutes.

6 Servings: 104 Calories per Serving; 0 Fat; 0 Cholesterol; 0 Saturated Fat.

Food Exchanges: 1-1/2 fruit.

Pumpkin Pie

Crust

2 Tbs. low-fat margarine
6 double graham crackers

Prepare crust by rolling graham crackers into crumbs, and mix with soft margarine. Spread evenly in eight-inch pie pan.

Filling

> 2 cups canned pumpkin
> 1/4 cup egg substitute
> 1 egg white
> 1/2 cup canned evaporated skim milk
> 2 Tbs. sugar
> 1 tsp. Sweet'n Low
> 1 tsp. cinnamon
> 1/8 tsp. nutmeg
> 1/8 tsp. allspice
> 1/8 tsp. salt

Mix all ingredients together. Beat at low speed with an electric beater or hand beater until mixture is well blended.

Pour into prepared graham cracker crust. Bake in pre-heated 350° oven for about 40 or 45 minutes. Test by inserting a knife. If knife comes out clean, the pie is done.

Topping

> 1 cup canned evaporated skim milk
> 1/2 tsp. sweetener
> 1/2 tsp. vanilla extract

Place milk in a small deep bowl and put in the freezer compartment until ice crystals form. Mix with electric beater at high speed until peaks form. Add sweetener and vanilla and mix with the electric beater. Make this up immediately before serving. Let someone else clear the table while you whip the cream. It is very important that this type of 'whipped cream' be served immediately because it retains its whipped state for only a short time—then it returns to its original state of canned milk, except now it will have vanilla and sweetener in it, which might taste rather strange if accidentally used later in a cream sauce or casserole.

8 Servings: 127 Calories per Serving; 4 grams Fat; 1 mg. Cholesterol; 1 gram Saturated Fat.

Food Exchanges: 1 bread; 1 fat.

Pumpkin–Rum Custard

1/3 cup sugar
1 cup canned evaporated skim milk
1 tsp. Sweet'n Low
1 tsp. rum extract
1 cup canned pumpkin
1/4 cup frozen egg substitute

In a skillet, caramelize 1/3 cup sugar by melting it over medium heat until it is light brown and syrupy. Pour at once into 4 custard cups sprayed with vegetable cooking spray.

In a saucepan, scald evaporated milk. Stir in sweetener, rum extract, and pumpkin. Beat some of this mixture into egg substitute. Then pour egg mixture into saucepan and beat by hand until well blended.

Pour pumpkin mixture into custard cups. Put custard cups in shallow baking pan filled with water to within 3/4" of top of cups.

Bake in pre-heated 325° oven for 45 minutes. Test at 35 to 40 minutes by inserting a knife; if it comes out clean, the custard is done. Refrigerate overnight. Take out of refrigerator a few minutes before serving. Run a knife around sides of each cup to loosen custard. Invert onto individual dessert plates.

4 Servings: 151 Calories per Serving; 2 grams Fat; 3 mg. Cholesterol; 0.5 grams Saturated Fat.

Food Exchanges: 1 bread; 1/2 fat; 1/2 milk.

——— Pumpkin Vanilla Pudding ———

Your family will never guess that this is a light dessert because it tastes so good and rich.

> 1 can pumpkin (16 oz.)
> 1 pkg. vanilla pudding mix (0.9 oz.), sugar-free instant
> 1 cup Cool Whip, Lite
> 1 cup skim milk
> 1 tsp. pumpkin pie spice

Mix pumpkin, instant vanilla pudding mix, and pumpkin pie spice. Add skim milk and beat with hand mixer. Fold in one cup of Cool Whip, Lite. Pour into custard cups or parfait glasses and chill in the refrigerator for a couple of hours.

Topping

> 1/2 cup canned evaporated skim milk
> 1/2 tsp. vanilla extract
> 2 pkts. sweetener
> Nutmeg

Make topping by pouring canned evaporated skim milk in a small deep mixing bowl and placing it in the freezing compartment of the refrigerator for 30 or 45 minutes, until ice crystals form. Take out just before serving. Beat at high speed with electric beater until peaks form. Add sweetener and vanilla extract. Put a swirl of dessert topping on each serving. Sprinkle a light dusting of nutmeg on top.

6 Servings: 104 Calories per Serving; 4 grams Fat; 2 mg. Cholesterol; 3 grams Saturated Fat.

Food Exchanges: 1/2 bread; 1/2 fat; 1/2 milk.

Rice Pudding

Rice pudding was a favorite "everyday" dessert of my childhood. It was not something we had for Sunday dinner with fried chicken and the Baptist preacher.

In deference to my mother, and to Alice Evett, my editor, who has picked those little brown things out of rice pudding all her life, I am omitting the raisins. You may add two tablespoons to the whole bit. Then you must add 12 calories to each serving. You may also sprinkle a dash of nutmeg or allspice over it.

> 1 cup cooked rice
> 1/4 cup frozen egg substitute
> 1/2 cup skim milk
> 1/8 tsp. salt
> 1/4 tsp. lemon extract
> 1/2 tsp. vanilla extract
> 1/2 tsp. sugar substitute
> 2 Tbs. sugar

Fold skim milk and beaten egg substitute into cooked rice. Add sugar, sugar substitute, lemon extract, and salt. Spray a small casserole pan with vegetable cooking spray. Pour in the mixture. Bake in 375° oven for 20 minutes.

4 Servings: 121 Calories per Serving; 2 grams Fat; 1 mg. Cholesterol; 0.3 grams Saturated Fat.

Food Exchanges: 1 bread; 1/2 milk.

Spanish Crême

1 envelope unflavored gelatin
1/4 cup cold water
1-1/2 tsp. sugar substitute
1-1/2 cups skim milk
1/4 cup egg substitute
2 egg whites
1/4 tsp. salt
2 tsp. grated orange rind
1 tsp. vanilla extract

Soften gelatin in cold water 5 minutes. Scald milk. Add salt, orange rind, and softened gelatin to egg substitute and beat slightly. Slowly add scalded milk, stirring until well blended. Cook slowly in double boiler, stirring constantly, until mixture coats a spoon. Cool slightly. Add sweetener and vanilla. Pour into a bowl. Chill until slightly thickened.

Beat egg whites until stiff. Fold into mixture. Pour into mold or sherbet dishes. Chill until firm.

6 Servings: 52 Calories per Serving; 1 gram Fat; 1 mg. Cholesterol; 0.3 grams Saturated Fat.

Food Exchanges: 2/3 milk.

Spicy Tapioca Cream

2 egg whites
1/4 cup frozen egg substitute, thawed
2 Tbs. sugar
7 pkts. Sweet'n Low
3 cups skim milk
1/3 cup quick-cooking tapioca
2 more Tbs. sugar
1 Tbs. cocoa
1/4 tsp. cinnamon
1/8 tsp. nutmeg
1/8 tsp. allspice
Dash of ground cloves
1/4 tsp. salt
1-1/2 tsp. vanilla extract

Beat egg whites until soft peaks form. Gradually add 2 Tbs. sugar. Continue beating until stiff peaks are formed. Set aside.

Combine egg substitute with milk in saucepan. Stir in tapioca. Mix 2 Tbs. sugar with cocoa, spices, Sweet'n Low, and salt. Add to mixture. Bring to a full boil over medium heat, stirring constantly. Do not over cook. Pudding will be thin.

Remove from heat. Gradually add a small amount of tapioca mixture to beaten egg whites, stirring constantly. Then quickly blend in remaining mixture and vanilla extract. Cool. Stir after about 15 minutes. Spoon into serving dishes. Chill thoroughly. To serve, top each with a dollop (1 Tbs.) of whipped dessert topping. (See Icebox Pumpkin Parfait.)

6 Servings: 145 Calories per Serving; 3 grams Fat; 5 mg. Cholesterol; 1 gram Saturated Fat.

Food Exchanges: 1/2 bread; 1/2 fruit; 1/2 milk.

Strawberry Rice Whip

1 banana
3/4 cup instant rice
2 Tbs. sugar
1/2 tsp. sweetener
1 (3 oz.) pkg. strawberry Jello, sugar-free
3/4 cup water
1 cup boiling water

Cook instant rice as per directions on package. Blend banana, sugar, sweetener, cool water, and cooked rice until smooth and creamy. Dissolve gelatin in boiling water. Add to blended mixture and chill. When mixture has congealed slightly, whip with electric beater until light and fluffy. This is such a pretty dessert that no one will suspect that the calories have been taken out.

6 Servings: 79 Calories per Serving; 0 Fat; 0 Cholesterol; 0 Saturated Fat.

Food Exchanges: 1/2 bread; 1/2 fat.

Sweet Potato Pudding

3 cups sweet potatoes, grated
2 Tbs. Butter Buds, mixed in water according to
    directions
1/4 cup egg substitute
1-/2 cups skim milk
2 Tbs. sugar
1-1/4 tsp. Sweet'n Low
1 tsp. nutmeg
1/2 cup orange juice

Grate sweet potatoes. Beat egg substitute and milk; add sugar and sweetener, Butter Buds, orange juice, and nutmeg. Mix with potatoes. Pour into 1-quart baking dish sprayed with vegetable cooking spray. Bake in pre-heated 350° oven for about 25 minutes.

8 Servings: 180 Calories per Serving; 2 grams Fat; 1 mg. Cholesterol; 0.5 Saturated Fat.

Food Exchanges: 2-1/3 breads.

———————— Tapioca Pudding ————————

1/4 cup egg substitute
4 cups skim milk, scalded
1/3 cup tapioca
1/4 cup sugar
1/2 tsp. sugar substitute
1/4 tsp. salt
2 egg whites, stiffly beaten
1 tsp. vanilla extract

In a saucepan, mix egg substitute with small amount of milk. Add tapioca and sugar, sweetener, salt, and remaining milk. Bring to a boil, stirring constantly. Remove from heat (mixture will be thin). Gradually fold hot mixture into stiffly-beaten egg whites. Add vanilla and chill thoroughly. You may spoon frozen peaches, canned apricots, sliced bananas, mandarin oranges, or chocolate sauce (see page 207) over the tapioca pudding at the time of serving. Be sure to add the calorie count of topping to the amount listed below.

I read somewhere that Tapioca Pudding was Lyndon Johnson's favorite dessert. Sorry I do not know which was his favorite topping.

8 Servings: 103 Calories per Serving; 1 gram Fat; 2 mg. Cholesterol; 0.3 grams Saturated Fat.

Food Exchanges: 1/2 meat; 1/2 bread; 1/2 milk.

Appetizers

APPETIZERS

It is not an accident that I have included only a few recipes for appetizers. You and I know that snacking on finger food is a dangerous habit for weight-problem persons. We cannot stop with one peanut, two peanuts, or three dozen peanuts once we get started.

Use these recipes for dips if you must, but be very careful about the crackers that you serve. Four saltines will cost you 50 calories. Best you use celery sticks or other raw vegetables. Better still, serve an attractive platter of cut-up raw vegetables with a low-calorie prepared dressing for a dip. Or serve small chunks of fresh fruit. My brother-in-law Gene has an aversion to dips. He can't believe that in our germ-conscious society, intelligent people will sit around and dip their half-eaten crackers into the same bowl with twenty other people.

It is quite acceptable to serve popcorn as company fare. Be sure that it is air popped, without butter or oil. You may want to sprinkle a little Molly McButter or another butter-flavored powder on the popcorn. You can have a cupful of plain popcorn for only 25 calories. A cupful of popcorn just might take the edge off your craving for food.

Clam Dip

1 can (7 oz.) minced clams
1/4 small onion
1/4 tsp. salt
6 oz. cottage cheese, low-fat
6 drops Tabasco sauce

Place all ingredients in electric blender. Cover and blend until smooth. Serve with celery sticks.

8 Servings of 2 Tbs. each: 28 Calories per Serving; 1 Fat; 16 mg. Cholesterol; 0.2 grams Saturated Fat.

Food Exchanges: 1/2 meat.

——————— Cottage Cheese Dip ———————

2 cups cottage cheese, low-fat
2 Tbs. skim milk
2 Tbs. sour cream, Pet's Artificial (25 calories per Tbs.)
1/2 tsp. grated onion
2 tsp. lemon juice
1/2 tsp. garlic powder
1/4 tsp. salt

Blend all ingredients in an electric blender until smooth. Makes 2 cups of basic dip. Be sure to have plenty of raw vegetable sticks, and keep the crackers and chips out of sight.

16 Servings of 2 Tbs. each: 26 Calories per Serving; 0 Fat; 0 Cholesterol; 0.3 grams Saturated Fat.

Food Exchanges: 1/2 meat.

Crabmeat Dip

4 Tbs. low-fat plain yogurt
I tsp. lemon juice
I cup flaked crabmeat
I Tbs. horseradish

Place all ingredients in electric blender, and blend until smooth. Makes one cup.

8 Servings of 2 Tbs. each: 22 Calories per Serving; I gram Fat; 17 mg. Cholesterol; 0.15 grams Saturated Fat.

Food Exchanges: 1/2 meat.

Oven-Fried Mushrooms

1/2 cup flour
1/2 tsp. paprika
9 slices melba toast (made into crumbs), 150 calories
1/4 cup Parmesan cheese
2 tsp. dried basil
1/4 cup egg substitute
I egg white
2 Tbs. skim milk
I pkg. fresh mushrooms
I Tbs. low-fat margarine

In brown paper bag, combine flour and paprika. In another brown bag, combine crumbs, cheese, and basil. Beat egg white until stiff and fold into egg substitute and milk. Shake mushrooms in flour mixture and dip in egg mixture. Then shake in crumb mixture to coat mushrooms.

Arrange mushrooms, cap-side down, on cookie sheet which has been sprayed with vegetable cooking spray. Drizzle lightly with melted margarine. Serve with Dipping Sauce (see below). Makes about 24 appetizers.

8 Servings of 3 mushrooms each: 95 Calories per Serving; 3 grams Fat; 3 mg. Cholesterol; 0.9 grams Saturated Fat.

Food Exchanges: 1 bread; 1/2 vegetable; 1/2 fat.

Dipping Sauce

1/4 cup low-fat yogurt
1 Tbs. mayonnaise, reduced calorie, cholesterol free
1 Tbs. Dijon-style mustard
1 tsp. horseradish
1 Tbs. chopped parsley

8 Servings: 12 Calories per Serving; 1 gram Fat; 1 mg. Cholesterol; 0.7 Saturated Fat.

Food Exchanges: Free.

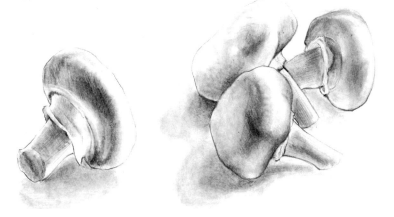

Shrimp Dip

1 cup boiled shrimp
2 Tbs. chili sauce
2 Tbs. mayonnaise, reducd calorie, cholesterol free
Dash of Tabasco sauce
Dash of salt
2 tsp. lemon juice
1 Tbs. onion, finely chopped

Place all ingredients in electric blender. Blend until smooth. Use as a party dip, but watch those crackers!

Makes 1-1/3 cups, or 21 tablespoons. 2 Tbs. constitute a Serving: 34 Calories per serving; 1 gram Fat; 45 mg. Cholesterol; .06 grams Saturated Fat.

Food Exchanges: 1/2 meat.

Beverages

BEVERAGES

In this chapter you will find recipes for several special beverages. Hard as I tried, however, I could not come up with a low-cal or even a high-cal beverage that is as good to drink or as good for you as that which the good Lord created on the First Day. After a few thousand years, the City Water Department had to doctor it up a bit. Well, maybe Ozarka or some other water bottling company doctored up *your* drinking water. Whether you drink it from the tap or from a jug, 'cool, clear water' is the perfect drink and should be consumed in the amount of eight 8-ounce glasses every day. We're talking about two quarts, or one half gallon of water per day. The only way I can keep up with that amount is to measure out two quarts of water in a pitcher or bottle each day and watch the water level recede.

These eight glasses of water are in addition to your coffee and tea. Most diet counselors suggest limiting tea and coffee to one or two cups or glassses per day.

Ice tea has always been considered a southern drink. In *Steel Magnolias*, Dolly called ice tea the "house wine of the South." But no more. My yuppie son, Terry, tells me that ice tea has taken the place of martinis in the 'three-martini lunch' for young executives back East.

It seems to me that the beverage industry has taken the lead through the years in taking the calories out of some of its products, thus giving the consumer choices in relation to calories and caffeine. There are sugar-free colas, ice tea, lemonade, Tang, and chocolate drink mixes.

The dairy industry has been juggling the fat content of milk for a long time. When I was a girl back on the farm, it was my job to turn the milk separator and to feed the skim milk to the calves, too soon weaned from their mother's teat. We poured the fresh milk in this contraption, turned the crank, and the cream came out one spout and the 'blue john' (skimmed milk) came out the other spout. You see, my dad sold cream to the dairies. My mother saved out the whole milk for her family use. We did give some of the skim milk to the neighbors, whose one cow had 'gone dry.' The neighbor's skinny children grew up without weight problems. My mother's plump rosy-cheeked children grew up to be fat.

I hope you will try some of these recipes which should add a little zest to your life. I'm particularly proud of the Russian Tea mix which "doesn't have a calorie in a carload." Serve it at your next tea or bridge party. Your friends will love it.

—————— Brandee Cocktail ——————

1 can (12 oz.) low-calorie cream soda
2 Tbs. nonfat dry milk
2 tsp. brandy flavoring
2 pkts. sweetener
1 cup crushed ice

Blend all ingredients in electric blender for 30 seconds. Serve in cocktail glasses.

2 Servings: 16 Calories per Serving; 0 Fat; 0 Cholesterol; 0 Saturated Fat.

Food Exchanges: Free.

——————— Cappucino Whip ———————

1 cup iced coffee, strong
1 tsp. chocolate extract
1/3 cup nonfat dry milk
2 pkts. sweetener
1/2 tsp. vanilla extract
1/2 tsp. brandy extract
6 or 7 ice cubes, crushed

Combine all ingredients in an electric blender. Blend together at high speed until light and frothy.

2 Servings: 53 Calories per Serving; 0 Fat; 4 mg. Cholesterol; 0 Saturated Fat.

Food Exchanges: 1/2 milk.

——————— Chocolate Soda ———————

1 can (12 oz.) diet chocolate soda
1/2 tsp. vanilla extract
1/2 tsp. chocolate extract
1/2 cup nonfat dry milk
2 pkts. sweetener
7 or 8 ice cubes

Blend ingredients together in electric blender at high speed. Add ice cubes one at a time.

2 Servings: 73 Calories per Serving; 0 Fat; 6 mg. Cholesterol; 0 Saturated Fat.

Food Exchanges: 1 milk.

Creamy Soda

I can (12 oz.) sugar-free cream soda
3/4 cup canned evaporated skim milk
I tsp. vanilla extract
2 pkts. sweetener
5 or 6 ice cubes

Combine all ingredients in electric blender. Blend at high speed for 30 seconds.

3 Servings: 55 Calories per Serving; 0 Fat; 8 mg. Cholesterol; 0 Saturated Fat.

Food Exchanges: 1/2 milk.

Egg Nog

1/4 cup frozen egg substitute
I pkt. Sweet'n Low
Dash of salt
3/4 cup canned evaporated skim milk
3/4 cup water
I tsp. vanilla extract
1/2 tsp. nutmeg

Place ingredients in electric blender and blend until smooth. Serve slightly chilled.

2 Servings: 135 Calories per Serving; 4 grams Fat; 4 mg. Cholesterol; 0.8 grams Saturated Fat.

Food Exchanges: I milk; 1/2 meat; 1/2 fat.

Mock Brandy Alexander

I cup water
2/3 cup nonfat dry milk
3 tsp. brandy extract
8 pkts. sweetener
1/2 tsp. nutmeg
7 or 8 ice cubes

Combine water, nonfat dry milk, brandy extract, and sweetener in electric blender. Add ice cubes one at a time, while blender is on high speed. Blend until light and frothy. Pour into stemmed glasses and sprinkle nutmeg on top.

4 Servings: 50 Calories per Serving; 0 Fat; 2 mg. Cholesterol; 0 Saturated Fat.

Food Exchanges: 1/2 milk.

Mock Strawberry Daiquiri

I cup frozen strawberries, unsweetened
2 Tbs. lime juice
3 pkts. sweetener
I tsp. rum flavoring
I cup crushed ice

Place ingredients in electric blender and blend on high until well blended. Serve in cocktail glasses with one strawberry on top of each.

2 Servings: 35 Calories per Serving; 0 Fat; 0 Cholesterol; 0 Saturated Fat.

Food Exchanges: 1/2 fruit.

Mock Piña Colada

1 sliced banana
1 cup crushed pineapple, unsweetened
1/4 tsp. coconut extract
1/4 tsp. rum extract
1 cup evaporated skim milk
2 pkts. Sweet'n Low
1 cup crushed ice

Place ingredients in an electric blender, and beat on high speed until consistency of a snow cone.

4 Servings: 98 Calories per Serving; 0 Fat; 3 mg. Cholesterol; 0 Saturated Fat.

Food Exchanges: 1 fruit; 1/2 milk.

Mock Hot Buttered Rum

1 cup skim milk
1 pkt. sweetener
1/2 tsp. rum extract
1/2 tsp. butter flavoring
1/4 tsp. nutmeg

Heat milk to point just before boiling. Add sweetener, rum extract, butter flavoring. Stir. Sprinkle cinnamon on top. This is great to warm you up when you come in from the cold—almost as good as the real thing.

One Serving: 100 Calories per Serving; 0.4 Fat; 4 mg. Cholesterol; 0.3 grams Saturated Fat.

Food Exchanges: 1 skim milk.

Orange–Apple Cooler

3 cups orange juice
1 cup apple, sliced and cored
1 cup crushed ice

Place ingredients in electric blender and blend at high speed until thoroughly mixed.

4 Servings: 99 Calories per Serving; 0 Fat; 0 Cholesterol; 0 Saturated Fat.

Food Exchanges: 1 fruit.

Orange Yogurt Smoothie

1/2 cup plain yogurt
3 oz. canned frozen orange juice, undiluted and
*   unthawed*
1/2 cup water
3 pkts. sweetener
1-1/2 tsp. vanilla extract
7 or 8 ice cubes

Place all ingredients in electric blender and blend at high speed until smooth and creamy.

2 Servings: 116 Calories per Serving; 0 Fat; 1 mg. Cholesterol; 0 Saturated Fat.

Food Exchanges: 1 fruit; 1/2 milk.

Piña Colada Shake

1 cup skim milk
1/4 cup nonfat dry milk
1/2 cup water
1 banana, ripe
1/8 tsp. pineapple extract
1/8 tsp. coconut extract
1/4 tsp. rum extract
7 or 8 ice cubes

Mix powdered milk with water and blend. Cut up banana. Place all ingredients in electric blender, and blend until consistency of a milk shake.

2 Servings: 126 Calories per Serving; 1 gram Fat; 4 mg. Cholesterol; 0.3 Saturated Fat.

Food Exchanges: 1 fruit; 1 milk.

Russian Tea Mix

This makes a nice non-alcoholic drink to serve in the wintertime, especially around the holidays. Make up the mix and keep on hand to serve when friends and relatives drop by. It is also good to package and add to Christmas baskets for friends who are concerned about gaining weight during the winter holidays.

4 tsp. sugar-free Tang (one tub)
4 tsp. Country-Time Lemonade, sugar-free (one tub)
4 tsp. instant tea, unsweetened
1 tsp. cinnamon, ground

1/2 tsp. allspice
2 pkts. sweetener

Mix all ingredients. Store in a covered jar. When ready to serve, put one teaspoon of the powder in a cup, and fill with boiling water.

22 Servings: 6 Calories per Serving.

Food Exchanges: Free.

———— Strawberry Supreme ————

1 cup skim milk
1 cup frozen strawberries (no sugar added),
    partially defrosted
1/2 cup ice cream, reduced calories (90 calories
    per 1/2 cup)
2 pkts. Sweet'n Low

Place ingredients in electric blender and mix until thoroughly blended.

2 Servings: 118 Calories per Serving; 0 Fat; 2 mg. Cholesterol; 0 Saturated Fat.

Food Exchanges: 1/2 bread; 1/2 fruit; 1/2 milk.

——— Theresa's Wassail, Decaloried ———

1 pint brewed tea, unsweetened
1 qt. Ocean Spray Low-Calorie Cranapple Juice
1 cup orange juice

10 whole cloves
2 cinnamon sticks, 2"
1/2 tsp. orange peel, dried
4 lemon slices
5 pkts. sweetener

Mix all ingredients except sweetener and bring to a beginning boil. Simmer for about ten minutes. Add sweetener. Serve hot.

9 Servings of 6-1/3 oz. servings: 36 Calories per Serving; 0 Fat; 0 Cholesterol; 0 Saturated Fat.

Food Exchanges: Free.

——————— Tomato Cocktail ———————

2 cups tomato juice, chilled
1 carrot, peeled and sliced
1 tsp. lemon juice
1 pinch black pepper
1/4 tsp. Worcestershire sauce

Place ingredients in electric blender and blend until smooth.

2 Servings: 59 Calories per Serving; 0 Fat; 0 Cholesterol; 0 Saturated Fat.

Food Exchanges: 2 vegetables.

Virgin Mary Mix

If you make this into a Bloody Mary, add 95 Calories per 1-1/2 oz. of vodka.

> 1 can (46 oz.) tomato juice
> 1 can (10 oz.) beef broth
> 2 cups orange juice
> 5 Tbs. lemon juice
> 5 Tbs. Worcestershire sauce
> 2 dashes of Tabasco sauce
> 1 tsp. salt
> Celery sticks for stirrers

Makes 1/2 Gallon: 3/4 cup per Serving: 10-1/2 Servings: 52 Calories per Serving: 0 Fat; 0 Cholesterol; 0 Saturated Fat.

Food Exchanges: 1/2 fruit.

Wake-Up Cocktail

> 2 cups orange juice, unsweetened
> 1 cup pineapple juice, unsweetened
> 1/2 cup apple slices
> 1 ripe banana
> 1 carrot, chopped
> 1/2 cucumber
> 1 cup crushed ice

Place orange juice and pineapple juice in electric blender. Add other ingredients, blending to a smooth liquid. This is a great pick-me-up after a fun night, or after a hard day's work.

6 Servings: 90 Calories per Serving; 0 Fat; 0 Cholesterol; 0 Saturated Fat.

Food Exchanges: 1-1/2 fruit.

Calorie Chart
for Cooks

— CALORIE CHART FOR COOKS —

We have prepared this calorie and cholesterol chart as a convenience for cooks. As you can see, we have included fats, saturated fats, and sodium, as well as calories and cholesterol. We want to remind you that the cholesterol count can be misleading. It is the saturated fats and the hydrogenated fats which can cause cholesterol build-up in the body. We have included sodium count for the benefit of those of you who need or want to prepare low sodium meals.

We have not included prepared foods, such as pies, cakes, and casseroles. We have included some cereals and canned foods commonly used in the preparation of other dishes. In cooked food, the calculation is based on no fats or salt added. In canned food, the calculation is based on regular canned food, not salt free.

The information for this chart came from *Home and Garden Bulletin* #72, "Nutritive Value of Food", by the U.S. Department of Agriculture, and by the label declaration of some specific products.

Calorie Count of Common Ingredients

	Quantity	Calories	Fat Grams	Saturated Fat Grams	Cholesterol Mg.	Sodium Mg.
Dairy Products						
Cheese						
Cheddar	1 oz.	115	9	6	30	176
Cottage (½% fat)	1 cup	125	1	0.4	10	19
Parmesan, grated	1 Tbs.	25	2	1	4	93
Pasteurized process						
American	1 oz.	105	9	5.6	27	406
Milk						
1%	1 cup	100	3	1.6	10	123
Skim	1 cup	85	Tr.	0.3	4	126
Buttermilk	1 cup	100	2	1.3	9	257
Dried non-fat	1 cup	245	Tr.	0.3	12	373
Sour Cream	1 Tbs.	25	3	1.6	5	6
Whipped Frozen Topping	1 Tbs.	15	1	0.9	0	1
Yogurt, plain (non-fat						
milk)	1 cup	125	Tr.	0.3	4	174
Eggs						
Large, raw	1 egg	80	6	1.7	274	69
White	1 white	15	Tr.	0	0	50
Yolk	1 yolk	65	6	1.7	272	8
Fats						
Butter, stick	½ cup	810	92	57.1	247	933[1]
	1 Tbs.	100	11	7.1	31	116
Lard	1 cup	1,850	205	80.4	195	0
Margarine, stick	½ cup	810	91	17.9	0	1,066[2]
Margarine, imitation (40%						
fat) soft	8 oz.	785	88	17.5	0	2,178[2]
	1 Tbs.	50	5	1.1	0	134
Vegetable shortening	1 cup	1,810	205	51.3	0	0
	1 Tbs.	115	13	3.3	0	0
Oils, Salad or Cooking						
Corn	1 cup	1,925	218	27.7	0	0
	1 Tbs.	125	14	1.8	0	0

[1] For salted butter; unsalted contains 12 mg sodium per stick.

[2] For salted margarine.

	Quantity	Calories	Fat Grams	Saturated Fat Grams	Cholesterol Mg.	Sodium Mg.
Olive	I cup	1,910	216	29.2	0	0
	I Tbs.	125	14	1.9	0	0
Peanut	I cup	1,910	216	36.5	0	0
	I Tbs.	125	14	2.4	0	0
Safflower	I cup	1,925	218	19.8	0	0
	I Tbs.	125	14	1.3	0	0
Canola, Puritan[3]	I Tbs.	120	14	1	0	0
Soybean oil, hydrogenated	I cup	1,925	218	32.5	0	0

Salad Dressings

	Quantity	Calories	Fat Grams	Saturated Fat Grams	Cholesterol Mg.	Sodium Mg.
Blue Cheese	I tsp.	75	8	1.5	3	164
French						
Regular	I Tbs.	85	9	1.4	0	188
Low calorie	I Tbs.	25	2	0.2	0	306
Italian						
Regular	I Tbs.	80	9	1.3	0	162
Low calorie	I Tbs.	5	Tr.	Tr.	0	136
Mayonnaise						
Regular	I Tbs.	100	11	1.7	8	80
Imitation	I Tbs.	35	3	0.5	4	75
Miracle Whip, Light[3]	I Tbs.	45	4	1	0	115
Thousand Island						
Regular	I Tbs.	60	6	1	4	112
Low calorie	I Tbs.	25	2	0.2	2	150

Fruits and Fruit Juices

	Quantity	Calories	Fat Grams	Saturated Fat Grams	Cholesterol Mg.	Sodium Mg.
Apple, 2¾″ diam.	I apple	80	Tr.	0.1	0	Tr.
Applesauce, unsweetened	I cup	105	Tr.	Tr.	0	5
Apricots, raw	3	50	Tr.	Tr.	0	1
Juice pack	I cup	120	Tr.	Tr.	0	10
Dried, uncooked	I cup	310	1	Tr.	0	13
Avocado (2/lb.)	I	305	30	4.5	0	21
Banana, raw	I	105	1	0.2	0	1
Blackberries, raw	I cup	75	1	0.2	0	Tr.
Blueberries						
Raw	I cup	80	1	Tr.	0	9
Frozen, sweetened	I cup	185	Tr.	Tr.	0	2
Cantaloupe (5 in.)	½	95	1	0.1	0	24

[3] Declaration on label.

	Quantity	Calories	Fat Grams	Saturated Fat Grams	Cholesterol Mg.	Sodium Mg.
Cherries						
Sour, red pitted, canned, water-pkd	I cup	90	Tr.	0.1	0	17
Sweet, raw	10	50	I	0.1	0	Tr.
Cranberry juice, bottled, sweetened	I cup	145	Tr.	Tr.	0	10
Cranberry sauce canned, sweetened	I cup	420	Tr.	Tr.	0	80
Dates, whole	10	230	Tr.	0.1	0	2
Figs, dried	10	475	2	0.4	0	21
Fruit cocktail, juice packed	I cup	115	Tr.	Tr.	0	10
Grapefruit, raw, 3¾" diameter	½	40	Tr.	Tr.	0	Tr.
Grapefruit juice, can, unsweetened	I cup	95	Tr.	Tr.	0	2
Grapes						
Thompson, seedless	10	35	Tr.	0.1	0	I
Tokay and Emperor	10	40	Tr.	0.1	0	I
Grapejuice, sweetened canned or bottled	I cup	155	Tr.	0.1	0	8
Kiwifruit, raw	I	45	Tr.	Tr.	0	4
Lemons	I	15	Tr.	Tr.	0	I
Lemon juice						
Raw	I cup	60	Tr.	Tr.	0	2
Canned or bottled	I cup	50	I	0.1	0	51
Lime juice						
Raw	I cup	65	Tr.	Tr.	0	2
Canned, unsweetened	I cup	50	I	0.1	0	39
Mangos, raw, 1½/lb. with seed	I mango	135	I	0.1	0	4
Melon, honeydew, 6½" diam.	⅟₁₀ melon	45	Tr.	Tr.	0	13
Nectarines, raw	I	65	I	0.1	0	Tr.
Orange, raw, 2⅝"	I	60	Tr.	Tr.	0	Tr.
Orange juice						
Raw or frozen, dil.	I cup	110	Tr.	Tr.	0	2
Can, unsweetened	I cup	105	Tr.	Tr.	0	5
Papayas, raw ½" cube	I cup	65	Tr.	0.1	0	9

	Quantity	Calories	Fat Grams	Saturated Fat Grams	Cholesterol Mg.	Sodium Mg.
Peaches, raw						
Whole, 2½"	I	35	Tr.	Tr.	0	Tr.
Sliced	I cup	75	Tr.	Tr.	0	Tr.
Canned, juice pack	I cup	110	Tr.	Tr.	0	10
Dried, uncooked	I cup	380	I	0.1	0	11
Dried, cooked,						
unsweetened	I cup	200	I	0.1	0	11
Pears						
Bartlett, raw 2½"	I	100	I	Tr.	0	Tr.
Bosc, raw 2½"	I	85	I	Tr.	0	Tr.
D'Anjou, raw 3"	I	120	I	Tr.	0	Tr.
Can, juice pack	I cup	125	Tr.	Tr.	0	10
Pineapple						
Raw, diced	I cup	75	I	Tr.	0	2
Can, juice pack chunks	I cup	150	Tr.	Tr.	0	3
Can, juice pack sliced	I slice	35	Tr.	Tr.	0	I
Plums, raw, 2⅛"	I	35	Tr.	Tr.	0	Tr.
Prunes, dried						
Uncooked	5 large	115	Tr.	Tr.	0	2
Cooked, unsweetened,						
fruit and liquid	5 large	225	Tr.	Tr.	0	4
Raisins, uncooked	I cup	435	I	0.2	0	17
	1½ Tbs.	40	Tr.	Tr.	0	2
Raspberries, raw	I cup	60	I	Tr.	0	Tr.
Strawberries, raw whole	I cup	45	Tr.	Tr.	0	I
Tangerines, raw, 2⅜"						
diam.	I	35	Tr.	Tr.	0	I
Watermelon,						
4x8" wedge	I piece	155	2	0.3	0	10
Diced	I cup	50	I	0.1	0	3

Grain Products
Bread

	Quantity	Calories	Fat Grams	Saturated Fat Grams	Cholesterol Mg.	Sodium Mg.
Wheat	I slice	65	I	0.2	0	138
White, enriched	I slice	65	I	0.3	0	129
Bread crumbs	I cup	120	2	0.6	0	231
Corn hominy grits, cooked	I cup	145	Tr.	Tr.	0	0
Corn flakes	1¼ cup	110	Tr.	Tr.	0	351

	Quantity	Calories	Fat Grams	Saturated Fat Grams	Cholesterol Mg.	Sodium Mg.
Corn meal						
Nearly whole grain	1 cup	440	4	0.5	0	2.2
De-germed enriched	1 cup	500	2	0.2	0	1
Crackers						
Graham, plain 2½"						
square	2	60	1	0.4	0	86
Melba toast, plain	1	20	Tr.	0.1	0	44
Rye wafer 1⅞ x 3½"	2	55	1	0.3	0	115
Saltines	4	50	1	0.5	4	165
Wheat Thins	4	35	1	0.5	0	69
English muffins, plain,						
enriched	1	140	1	0.3	0	378
Macaroni, cooked	1 cup	155	1	0.1	0	1
Noodles, cooked	1 cup	200	2	0.5	50	3
Rice, cooked	1 cup	225	Tr.	0.1	0	0
Spaghetti, cooked	1 cup	155	1	0.1	0	1
Flour						
All-purpose,enriched						
Sifted	1 cup	420	1	0.2	0	2
Unsifted	1 cup	455	1	0.2	0	3
Buckwheat, sifted	1 cup	340	1	0.2	0	2
Cake flour	1 cup	350	1	0.2	0	2
Self-rising	1 cup	440	1	0.2	0	1,349
Whole wheat	1 cup	400	2	0.3	0	4
Legumes, Nuts, and Seeds						
Almonds, whole	1 oz.	165	15	1.4	0	3
Beans, dry, cooked,						
drained						
Great Northern	1 cup	210	1	0.1	0	13
Lima	1 cup	260	1	0.2	0	4
Navy	1 cup	225	1	0.1	0	13
Pinto	1 cup	265	1	0.1	0	3
Black-eyed peas	1 cup	190	1	0.2	0	20
Beans, canned pork and						
beans	1 cup	310	7	2.4	10	330
Lentils, dry cooked	1 cup	215	1	0.1	0	26
Mixed nuts, dry roasted	1 oz.	170	15	2.0	0	190
Peanut butter	1 Tbs.	95	8	1.4	0	75

	Quantity	Calories	Fat Grams	Saturated Fat Grams	Cholesterol Mg.	Sodium Mg.
Sesame seeds	1 Tbs.	45	4	0.6	0	3
Sunflower seeds	1 Tbs.	160	14	1.5	0	1
Tofu, 2½x2¾x1″	1	85	5	0.7	0	8
Walnuts, black	1 oz.	170	16	1.0	0	Tr.
Walnuts, English	1 oz.	180	18	1.6	0	3

Vegetables

	Quantity	Calories	Fat Grams	Saturated Fat Grams	Cholesterol Mg.	Sodium Mg.
Alfalfa seeds, raw, sprouted	1 cup	10	Tr.	Tr.	0	2
Artichokes, cooked, drained	1	55	Tr.	Tr.	0	79
Asparagus, green,						
Cooked, drained	1 cup	45	1	1	0	7
Spears ½″ diam.	4	15	Tr.	Tr.	0	2
Frozen	1 cup	50	1	0.2	0	7
Canned	4 spears	10	1	0.1	0	278
Bamboo shoots, canned, drained	1 cup	25	1	0.1	0	9
Bean sprouts						
Raw	1 cup	30	Tr.	Tr.	0	3
Cooked, drained	1 cup	25	Tr.	Tr.	0	12
Beans, Lima, frozen, cooked, drained	1 cup	170	1	0.1	0	90
Beans, Snap						
From raw	1 cup	45	Tr.	0.1	0	4
From frozen	1 cup	35	Tr.	Tr.	0	18
Canned, drained	1 cup	25	Tr.	Tr.	0	359
Beets						
Cooked, drained	1 cup	55	Tr.	Tr.	0	83
Canned, drained	1 cup	55	Tr.	Tr.	0	466
Black-eyed peas						
From raw	1 cup	180	1	0.3	0	7
Frozen	1 cup	225	1	0.3	0	9
Broccoli						
Raw	1 spear	40	1	0.1	0	41
Cooked, drained	1 spear	50	1	0.1	0	20
Cut up	1 cup	45	Tr.	0.1	0	17
Brussels sprouts, cooked, drained	1 cup	60	1	0.2	0	33

	Quantity	Calories	Fat Grams	Saturated Fat Grams	Cholesterol Mg.	Sodium Mg.
Cabbage, common var.						
Raw, shredded or sliced	I cup	15	Tr.	Tr.	0	13
Cooked, drained	I cup	30	Tr.	Tr.	0	29
Red, raw, shredded	I cup	20	Tr.	Tr.	0	8
Carrots						
Whole 7½x1⅛"	I	30	Tr.	Tr.	0	25
Grated	I cup	45	Tr.	Tr.	0	39
Cooked, from raw	I cup	70	Tr.	Tr.	0	103
Cooked, from frozen	I cup	55	Tr.	Tr.	0	86
Canned, sliced	I cup	35	Tr.	0.1	0	352
Cauliflower						
Raw, flowerets	I cup	25	Tr.	Tr.	0	15
Cooked, from raw	I cup	30	Tr.	0.1	0	8
From frozen	I cup	35	Tr.	0.1	0	32
Celery, pascal						
Raw, outer stalk	I stalk	5	Tr.	Tr.	0	35
Pieces, diced	I cup	20	Tr.	Tr.	0	106
Collards						
From raw	I cup	25	Tr.	0.1	0	36
From frozen	I cup	60	I	0.1	0	85
Corn, sweet, cooked						
From raw 5x1¾"	I ear	85	I	0.2	0	13
Kernels	I cup	135	Tr.	Tr.	0	8
Canned, creamstyle	I cup	185	I	0.2	0	730
Canned, whole kernel	I cup	165	I	0.2	0	571
Cucumber ⅛" thick (large 2⅛" diam, small 1¾" diam)	6 lrg or 8 sml slices	5	Tr.	Tr.	0	I
Eggplant, cooked steamed	I cup	25	Tr.	Tr.	0	3
Endive, curly	I cup	10	Tr.	Tr.	0	11
Kale, from raw, cooked, drained	I cup	40	I	0.1	0	30
Lettuce, iceberg						
6" head	I head	70	I	0.1	0	49
Chopped or shredded	I cup	5	Tr.	Tr.	0	5
Loose leaf, chopped	I cup	10	Tr.	Tr.	0	5
Mushrooms						
Raw, sliced	I cup	20	Tr.	Tr.	0	3
Canned, drained	I cup	35	Tr.	Tr.	0	663

	Quantity	Calories	Fat Grams	Saturated Fat Grams	Cholesterol Mg.	Sodium Mg.
Mustard greens, cooked,						
drained	I cup	20	Tr.	Tr.	0	22
Okra pods, 3x⅝" cooked	8 pods	25	Tr.	Tr.	0	4
Onions						
Raw, chopped	I cup	55	Tr.	0.1	0	3
Cooked	I cup	60	Tr.	0.1	0	17
Spring, ⅜" diam.	6 onions	10	Tr.	Tr.	0	I
Parsley	10 sprigs	5	Tr.	Tr.	0	4
Peas, edible pod, cooked,						
drained	I cup	65	Tr.	0.1	0	6
Peas, green						
Canned, strained	I cup	115	I	0.1	0	372
Frozen, cooked	I cup	125	Tr.	0.1	0	139
Pepper, bell (5/lb.)	I pepper	20	Tr.	Tr.	0	2
Potatoes						
Baked (2/lb. raw)						
with skin	I potato	220	Tr.	0.1	0	16
without skin	I potato	145	Tr.	Tr.	0	8
Boiled (3/lb. raw)	I potato	120	Tr.	Tr.	0	5
Pumpkin						
Cooked from raw,						
mashed	I cup	50	Tr.	0.1	0	2
Canned	I cup	85	Tr.	0.1	0	12
Radishes	4	5	Tr.	Tr.	0	4
Sauerkraut, canned, solid						
& liquid	I cup	45	Tr.	0.1	0	1,560
Spinach						
Raw, chopped	I cup	10	Tr.	Tr.	0	43
Cooked, drained						
From raw	I cup	40	Tr.	0.1	0	126
From frozen	I cup	55	Tr.	0.1	0	163
Canned drained	I cup	50	I	0.2	0	683
Squash, cooked						
Summer, all var., sliced,						
drained	I cup	35	I	0.1	0	2
Winter, all var., baked,						
cubes	I cup	80	I	0.3	0	2

	Quantity	Calories	Fat Grams	Saturated Fat Grams	Cholesterol Mg.	Sodium Mg.
Sweet potatoes						
Cooked (raw 5x2")						
Baked in skin, peeled	I potato	115	Tr.	Tr.	0	11
Boiled without skin	I potato	160	Tr.	Tr.	0	20
Canned, solid pack	I cup	260	I	0.1	0	191
Tomatoes						
Raw 2⅗" diam.	I tomato	25	Tr.	Tr.	0	10
Canned, solid & liq	I cup	50	Tr.	Tr.	0	391
Tomato juice, canned	I cup	40	Tr.	Tr.	0	881
Tomato products						
Paste[4]	I cup	220	2	0.3	0	170
Puree[4]	I cup	105	Tr.	Tr.	0	50
Sauce[5]	I cup	75	Tr.	0.1	0	1,482
Turnips, cooked	I cup	30	Tr.	Tr.	0	78
Turnip greens cooked,						
drained	I cup	30	Tr.	0.1	0	42
Vegetables, mixed						
Canned, drained	I cup	75	Tr.	0.1	0	243
Frozen	I cup	105	Tr.	Tr.	0	64
Water chestnuts						
Canned	I cup	70	Tr.	Tr.	0	11
Sugars and Sweets						
Honey, strained	I cup	1,030	0	0	0	17
	I Tbs.	65	0	0	0	I
Sugars						
Brown, pressed down	I cup	820	0	0	0	97
White, granulated	I cup	770	0	0	0	5
	I Tbs.	45	0	0	0	Tr.
	I packet	25	0	0	0	Tr.
Powdered, sifted,						
spooned into cup	I cup	385	0	0	0	2
Molasses, cane	2 Tbs.	85	0	0	0	38

[4] No salt added.
[5] Salt added.

	Quantity	Calories	Fat Grams	Saturated Fat Grams	Cholesterol Mg.	Sodium Mg.
Table syrup, corn and maple	2 Tbs.	122	0	0	0	19
Fish and Shellfish						
Clams						
Raw, meat only	3 oz.	65	1	0.3	43	102
Canned, drained	2 oz.	85	2	0.5	54	102
Crabmeat, canned	1 cup	135	3	0.5	135	1,350
Fresh[6]						
Flounder or Sole						
Baked without fat	3 oz.	80	1	0.3	59	101
Oysters, raw only (13–19 medium)	1 cup	160	4	1.4	120	175
Salmon						
Canned (pink) solid and liquid	3 oz.	120	5	0.9	34	443
Baked	3 oz.	140	5	1.2	60	55
Smoked	3 oz.	150	8	2.6	51	1,700
Shrimp						
Canned	3 oz.	100	1	0.2	128	1,955
Fresh[6]						
Tuna, canned, water-packed, white	3 oz.	135	1	0.3	48	468
Chicken						
Breast, roasted, flesh only	3 oz.	140	3	0.9	73	64
Drumstick, flesh only	1.6 oz.	75	2	0.7	41	42
Stewed, light and dark, chopped or diced	1 cup	250	9	2.6	116	98
Canned	5 oz.	235	11	3.1	88	714
Frankfurter	1 frank	115	9	2.5	45	616
Liver, cooked	1 liver	30	1	0.4	126	10
Turkey						
Roasted, dark meat 2½x1⅝x¼″	4 pieces	160	6	2.1	72	67
Roasted, light meat 4x2x¼″	2 pieces	135	3	0.9	59	54

[6] Information not available.

	Quantity	Calories	Fat Grams	Saturated Fat Grams	Cholesterol Mg.	Sodium Mg.
Light and dark, chopped	I cup	240	7	2.3	105	98
Turkey ham (8 slices per 8 oz. pkg)	2 slices	75	3	1.0	32	565
Roast, frozen, boneless, lght/drk	3 oz.	130	5	1.6	45	578
Meat and Meat Products						
Beef, pot roast, chuck lean only	2.2 oz.	170	9	3.9	66	44
Beef, pot roast, bottom round	2.8 oz.	175	8	2.7	75	40
Ground beef						
Broiled patty, lean	3 oz.	230	16	6.2	74	65
Broiled patty, reg	3 oz.	245	18	6.9	76	70
Beef, oven cooked no liquid, lean	2.2 oz.	150	9	3.6	49	45
Steak, sirloin, broiled, lean only	2.5 oz.	150	6	2.6	64	48
Beef, corned, canned	3 oz.	185	10	4.2	80	802
Beef, dried	2.5 oz.	145	4	1.8	46	3,053
Lamb, cooked						
Chops (3/lb. with bone) broiled, lean only	2.3 oz.	140	6	2.6	60	54
Leg roast, lean only	2.6 oz.	140	6	2.4	65	50
Rib roasted, lean only	2 oz.	130	7	3.2	50	46
Pork						
Bacon, regular	3 slices	110	9	3.3	16	303
Bacon, Canadian	2 slices	85	4	1.3	27	711
Ham roasted, lean	2.4 oz.	105	4	1.3	37	902
Luncheon meat, ham	2 oz.	105	6	1.9	32	751
Pork, fresh cooked						
Chop, loin (3/lb.), broiled, lean only	2.5 oz.	165	8	2.6	84	56
Ham roasted, lean only	2.5 oz.	160	8	2.7	68	46
Rib roasted, lean only	2.5 oz.	175	10	3.4	56	33
Bologna, sliced	2 oz.	180	16	6.1	31	581
Brown & serve sausage	I link	50	5	1.7	9	105
Frankfurter (10/pkg)	I	145	13	4.8	23	504
Vienna sausage	I sausage	45	4	1.5	8	152

	Quantity	Calories	Fat Grams	Saturated Fat Grams	Cholesterol Mg.	Sodium Mg.
Veal, medium fat						
Cutlet	3 oz.	185	9	4.1	109	56
Miscellaneous Items						
Catsup, regular	I cup	290	I	0.2	0	2,845
	I Tbs.	15	Tr.	Tr.	0	156
Catsup, Weight Watchers[7]	I Tbs.	8	0	0	0	110
Chocolate, bitter or baking	I oz.	145	15	9.0	0	I
Egg Substitute[7]						
99% real egg product,						
¼ cup = I egg	¼ cup	25	0	0	0	80
Gelatin, dry	I env.	25	Tr.	Tr.	0	6
Gelatin, flavored Jello,						
Sugar Free[7], one						
serving	½ cup	8	0	0	0	60
Jicama, cubed[7]	I cup	20	0	0	0	unavailable
Mustard, prepared yellow	I tsp.	5	0	0	0	63
Pudding, Jello, Sugar						
Free[7], one serving,						
no milk	½ cup	25	0	0	0	320
Olives, canned						
Green	4 med	15	2	0.2	0	312
Ripe	3 sml	15	0.3	0.2	0	68
Pickles, cucumber						
Dill 3¾" long, 1¼"						
diam.	I pickle	5	Tr.	Tr.	0	928
Sweet gherkin, sml						
2½x¾"	I pickle	20	Tr.	Tr.	0	107
Relish, sweet	I Tbs.	20	Tr.	Tr.	0	107
Salt	I tsp.	0	0	0	0	2,132
Yeast, bakers, dry, active	I pkg	20	Tr.	Tr.	0	4
Weight Watchers Cream						
of Mushroom Soup[7]	10.5 can	90	2	unavailable		1,250
Weight Watchers Sour						
Cream[7]	I oz.	35	2	unavailable		40
Wheat germ[7]	I Tbs.	30	I	0	0	0
	I oz.	100	3	Tr.	0	0

[7] Declaration on label.